Land
TUSCANY
of art

Published and printed by

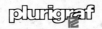

NARNI - TERNI

INDEX

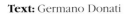

Text: Germano Donati
Photographs: Archivio Plurigraf - Arte e Immagini - Atlantide - Il Dagherrotipo -
Image Bank - Laura Ronchi - Max Mandel - Marka - Scala - Sie - Tony Stone - Tosi -
Tulli Federico- Vescovo Arnaldo
Aerial photos authorization: S.M.A. n° 402 del 16-05-1991 / S.M.A.° 01-161 del 17-04-1997 /
S.M.A. n° 01-26 del 14-01-1997 / M.D.A. n° 725-70

TUSCANY

The long curve of the Tyrrhenian coast and the backbone of the Appennines, the short range of the Apuan Alps and the picturesque coastal plain of the Maremma, dominated by Monte Amiata, define the contours of this region whose variety and magnificence of landscape are extraordinary. In the region's interior, the superb backdrop of the Appennines, where both the Arno and the Tiber have their source, dominates the landscape: broad and verdant valleys, rugged gorges, thick forests. Our every step is accompanied by the typical flora of Mediterranean countries: the vine, the olive and the cypress, a tree sacred to the Etruscans.

Twice, in the course of the millennia, Tuscany enjoyed a period of prodigious cultural efflorescence. Before the foundation of Rome, at a time when the Greek colonies flourished in southern Italy, the civilization of the Etruscans developed in this land. They founded the first Tuscan cities, some of which are still very much alive today.

After the year 1000 A.D., at the time of the long standing dispute between Papacy and Empire, Tuscany enjoyed a second and no less astonishing burst of civilization. Florence itself provided perhaps the most typical example of an evolution common to numerous Italian cities: the development, namely, that led from forms of communal democracy, through internecine strife, to the imposition of an absolute princedom - in the specific case of Florence, that of the Medici.

The last two centuries of the Middle Ages and the ensuing Renaissance

mark the happiest period in the history of Italian art. The city once again became the fulcrum of political and cultural life, and it was in this period that the urbanistic renewal of the major Tuscan cities was achieved. Wider circuits of walls, city gates and new streets were built, while the town fabric was distinguished by the twin centres of religious and political life: the great baptisteries, cathedrals and town halls were erected. At a later period, with the progressive concentration of wealth in the hands of a few powerful families, the private palaces of the nobility and family chapels were raised. In the figurative arts too a bourgeois view of life, logical and rational, was affirmed. The innovative painting of Giotto, responsive to nature, to the reality of things, opened the way to the pictorial achievements of the following century, just as the

great poetry of Dante Alighieri laid the foundations, in the Tuscan vernacular, of the Italian literary tongue. The individualism typical of the Renaissance found its full expression in the concept of genius. Leonardo da Vinci, both painter and scientist, embodied and personified the ideal of human versatility.

Thus, the countless marvels of nature are accompanied, in this region, by the indelible records of the past that testify so eloquently to the guiding role that Tuscany played in European culture in the period of her greatest splendour. In every corner, even the remotest, we find an ancient chapel, a hilltop castle, a palace, or a tower. Large cities, small cities, ancient cities: each has its treasure to show us, a fresco in the church, a piazza that has retained its original character; or celebrated museums, full of masterpieces, monumental cathedrals and palaces, massive walls and fortresses that attest to the artistic and economic splendour reached by these cities.

In our rapid itinerary through Tuscany, we will try to draw attention to the major artistic glories of each city, though without ignoring the essential aspects of the landscape, the main tourist resorts or the region's spas; leaving to the visitor the initiative to discover for himself the countless picturesque spots rich in immemorial peace and history which make this region so beautiful, and which no guidebook would ever be able to exhaust.

FLORENCE

HISTORICAL BACKGROUND

The first traces of civilization in the Arno valley, where the city of Florence now stands, date back to the Villanovan period (Iron Age). The Etruscans later ruled over the area; their domination persisted for several centuries, until they were eventually conquered by the Romans who founded a "municipium" with the auspicious name of "Florentia", with the aim of guarding the important ford over the Arno.

It was, after the fall of the Roman Empire, at first a feud of the marquesses of Tuscany, among whom Matilda of Canossa particularly distinguished herself at the time of the Investiture Contest between Pope Gregory VII and the Emperor Henry IV. Subsequently it became the theatre of violent struggles between the ancient aristocratic houses and the powerful class of the craft workers incorporated in the various guilds of arts and crafts· these rivalries gave rise to the two factions of the "Guelfs", favourable to the Pope, and the "Ghibellines", favourable to the Emperor.

Yet the ferocious civil strife that bedevilled Florence in the Middle Ages did not impede the political, cultural and economic development of the city which, by the close of the 13th century, had extended its rule over the rival cities of Siena, Arezzo and Pistoia. At the same time it witnessed the extra ordinary flowering of the arts expressed in the masterpieces of Cimabue, Giotto, Dante and Arnolfo di Cambio.

Meanwhile the political life of the city, as fertile and tormented as ever, saw the revolt of the common people against the magnates in the Ciompi Revolution (1378), the rise to power of the great banking houses destined to monopolise civic life, and the emergence of the Signoria (lordship) of the Medici under Cosimo the Elder (1389-1464); Medici rule over the city was to persist, despite periods of interruption, for almost three centuries.

Cosimo was succeeded by his son Piero di Cosimo (Piero the Gouty:

1416-1469), and then by his nephew Lorenzo, nicknamed the Magnificent (1449-1494), a patron, poet and politician of consummate skill who led Florence to the height of her splendour. A few years after the death of Lorenzo, the Republican faction, hostile to the rule of the patriciate and inflamed by the violent and passionate preaching of the Dominican friar Gerolamo Savonarola, gained the upper hand and entertained the hope, or rather the delusion, that it could resto re the life of the city to its original purity of custom that had, according to Savonarola, been vitiated by the taste for luxury, the thirst for profit, and a prevailing spirit of profanity and superficiality.

Restored to power, the Medici continued to govern the city, with the exception of one or two brief interregnums, until 1737, when the dynasty was finally extinguished on the death of Giangastone. Having in the meantime become a Grand-Duchy, Florence was then governed by the House of Lorraine, which retained it until the annexation of Florence and Tuscany to the Kingdom of Italy, whose capital Florence became in 1865.

From this time onwards the particular history of Florence was incorporated into the wider horizon of the history of Italy as a whole.

THE CATHEDRAL OF SANTA MARIA DEL FIORE

We begin our visit to the city by starting out from its most prestigious and important monument, the Cathedral or **Duomo** which is the third largest church in the world after St. Peter's in Rome and St. Paul's in London. It is situated in the religious centre of the city, formed by the union of two piazzas: the Piazza San Giovanni, with the **Baptistery**, **Archbishops' Palace** and the 14th century **Loggia del Bigallo**, and the Piazza del Duomo, which is occupied by the Cathedral itself, its adjacent Campanile or Bell-Tower, and the **Cathedral Museum**.

The original design of the Cathedral was the work of Arnolfo di Cambio, who began its construction in 1296. Following his death (1301), the work was continued by Giotto who was also responsible for the building of the adjacent Campanile.

From 1337 on the building of the Cathedral was continued by Francesco Talenti who made various modifications to Arnolfo's original plan, especially as regards the larger dimensions of the nave and aisles. The Cathedral was completed (apart from the dome) by Giovanni di Lapo Ghini in 1369. But it was not until 1887 that the existing facade was erected by Emilio de Fabris, the original facade begun by Arnolfo having long been demolished (1587).

of the Republic) Sir John Hawkwood (Paolo Uccello); and the similar fresco of the soldier of fortune Niccolò da Tolentino (Andrea del Castagno).

THE DOME OF FILIPPO BRUNELLESCHI

The dome is the masterpiece of Filippo Brunelleschi, who designed and completed it between 1420 and 1434. Enormous in size (45 metres in diameter at its base and 114 metres in height), the dome was erected without the use of the traditional scaffolding.

Brunelleschi used the socalled fishbone system with interlocking blocks of stone and bricks in such a way that the construction, which rose in progressively narrower concentric circles, could support itself. To give greater support and protection to the edifice, Brunelleschi conceived of a double dome with a cavity between the inner and outer faces, within which a stairway of 463 steps leads up to the terrace of the lantern. The frescoes inside the dome were begun by Vasari in 1470 and continued after his death, by Federico Zuccari; they illustrate the Last Judgement. At the beginning of the 16th century it was decided to decorate the external tambour of the dome with a marble arcaded balcony, which was supposed to run right round it. The commission was entrusted to Baccio d'Agnolo, who completed the first of the eight sides in 1508. Having consulted the authoritative opinion of Michelangelo who called the arcade "una gabbia da grilli" - a cage for crickets - the civic authorities ordered the cessation of the work.

INTERIOR: The majesty and grandeur of the Cathedral's exterior are repeated in the architecture of its interior, though This by contrast is essentially simple and austere in style. The Florentines always defended its simplicity so as to ensure that the church retained a particular solemnity and austerity. Its plan consists of a nave and twin aisles, separated by composite pillars, surmounted by gothic arches: Arnolfo's design has here been fairly faithfully respected. Important works of art by **Paolo Uccello** and **Andrea del Castagno** are also to be found in the basilica. Also fascinating is a visit to the crypt, in which a fresco of the Madonna attributed to the school of

Giotto is preserved; the altar consists of simple slabs of marble.

West wall (inner wall of the facade): the magnificent stained glass was designed by Lorenzo Ghiberti and Agnolo Gaddi. The prophets in the four corners of the clock-face were painted by Paolo Uccello.

RIGHT AISLE: bust of Brunelleschi (by Buggiano); statue of Isaiah (attributed to Donatello); bust of Giotto (Benedetto da Maiano); gothic water stoup (c. 1380); bust of Marsilio Ficino (sculpture by Ferruccio).

LEFT AISLE: entrance to the dome; painting of Dante explaining the Divine Comedy (Domenico di Michelino); fresco depicting the English soldier of fortune (and Captain

A view of the interior of the Duomo.

THE CAMPANILE OF GIOTTO

A magnificent example of Florentine gothic architecture, the **Campanile** or Bell-Tower also bears eloquent witness to the greatness of Giotto. He began its construction in 1334 and continued it until 1337 (the year of his death), by which time he had completed the first storey. The work was continued by Andrea Pisano, who constructed the whole of the second storey without the twinarched mullioned windows designed by his predecessor, thus dissociating himself from Giotto's original plan.

But in 1343 Francesco Talenti, on assuming the direction of the work, reverted to the original idea and faithfully respected it in erecting the Campanile's upper storeys, with the possible exception of its uppermost part, which is topped by a panoramic terrace in place of the pointed spire envisaged in the original design.

The whole of the lower storey is decorated with two rows of reliefs, the lower in hexagonal, the upper in rhomboidal compartments. Various artists contributed to the sculpting of these reliefs, including **Andrea Pisano**, **Alberto Arnoldi** and **Luca della Robbia**, completing a cycle that had been conceived by Giotto himself. The reliefs represent the liberal arts, the arts and crafts, the planets, the virtues and the sacraments.

THE BAPTISTERY

The Baptistery of San Giovanni, "*il mio bel San Giovanni*" as the immortal Dante apostrophised it in his Divine Comedy, was built over the remains of an Early Christian basilica in the 11th century, and represented the ancient Cathedral of Florence until 1128.

EXTERIOR: the octagonal plan, the exact and symmetrical distribution of volumes, the taste for pronouncedly geometric shapes, and the use of dichromatic marble revetments (white marble from Carrara and green serpentine from Prato), make this monument one of the most typical examples of Romanesque architecture in Tuscany.

INTERIOR: It echoes the octagonal plan of the exterior, and is topped by a cupola encrusted with beautiful Byzantine mosaics of the 12th-14th century, representing images of the Christian world with the Last Judgement on high; the imposing figure of Christ separates the blessed from the damned. The work is attributed to **Coppo di Marcovaldo**.

The exterior and interior of the Baptistery.

Byzantine mosaics in the dome - The images seen here are those of the Christian world, portraying the celestial hierarchy, the story of Genesis, the stories of Mary and Jesus, the stories of John the Baptist, and the Last Judgement. The artists must have worked on sheets of card provided by Florentine artists, among them Cimabue. The great figure of Christ in Judgment, more than eight metres in diameter, is attributed to the Florentine artist Coppo di Marcovaldo. Around the central lantern, the ranks of angels are portrayed.

THE GATE OF PARADISE

Of great artistic value are the Baptistery's three bronze doors which provide entrance and egress to it at its three cardinal points.

SOUTH DOOR: the most ancient of the three, it was sculpted by **Andrea Pisano**, disciple of Giotto, in 1330-36. Its 28 compartments represent Scenes from the Life of St. John the Baptist and allegories of the Theological and Cardinal Virtues.

NORTH DOOR: like wise divided into 28 compartments, it was sculpted with relief scenes by **Lorenzo Ghiberti** in 1425, aided by several of his pupils, including **Donatello** and **Paolo Uccello**. The reliefs represent Scenes from the New Testament, the Life of the Evangelists and the Doctors of the Church.

EAST DOOR: dubbed by Michelangelo the "Gate of Paradise", it represents the masterpiece of **Lorenzo Ghiberti**. The sculpting of its reliefs took 27 years (1425-1452); Ghiberti was assisted by his son Vittorio, Michelozzo and Benozzo Gozzoli. The ten large panels, covered with gold leaf, represent Scenes from the Old Testament. The door we see in the photograph is Ghiberti's original. The one now on view in the Baptistery is a faithful copy of it. The original is in the process of being restored; on completion, it will be housed in the Cathedral Museum, where some of the restored panels are already on show.

THE CATHEDRAL MUSEUM

The Cathedral Museum (Museo dell'Opera del Duomo) is situated in the piazza facing the north apse of the Cathedral. Housed in the former Palazzo Falconieri (n° 9 of the Piazza), it contains various works of sculpture removed from the **Campanile**, the **Cathedral** and the **Baptistery**, including the bronze reliefs from the Gates of Paradise we have already mentioned. From the Campanile come the hexagonal marble reliefs representing scenes of the life of Man, sculpted by **Andrea Pisano** and **Luca della Robbia**, and the 16 statues of prophets originally contained in its niches. Of these we may mention the Habakkuk and Jeremiah, sculpted by Donatello with uncompromising realism in 1436. From the Baptistery, apart from the silver altar, we may find the moving wooden Magdalen, again the work of Donatello.

And of the various works removed from the Cathedral we may mention the singinggalleries (or cantorie) of Donatello and Luca della Robbia and the Pietà of Michelangelo. The two singinggalleries are contemporaneous and were sculpted between 1431 and 1439. Yet they are very different in style: Donatello's dramatic, Luca's lyrical.

The Sala delle Formelle.

*Michelangelo's
Pietà.*

ORSANMICHELE

We return by the Via dei Calzaioli and so reach the original **Church of Orsanmichele**, otherwise known as **San Michele in Orto**, a magnificent gothic building erected over the ruins of the ancient loggia that served as the city's cornmarket; the loggia was enclosed and topped by two upper storeys by Simone Talenti in 1380. The twinaisled interior, supported by gothic arches, houses the beautiful marble **Tabernacle** erected by **Orcagna**.

Linked to the church by an overhead passageway is the **Palace of the Arte della Lana**, seat of the wool guild: one of the most powerful and richest of the medieval Florentine guilds. Close by is the **Loggia del Mercato Nuovo**: the loggia where the shopkeepers and bankers of medieval Florence once met. At its side is a bronze statue of a wild boar known as "Il Porcellino" (a copy of Tacca's original).

By way of the Via Pellicceria, we come to the **Palazzo Davanzati** in Via Porta Rossa, a Florentine noble residence of the 14th century, while behind the Loggia is the **Palazzo di Parte Guelfa**, originally built in the 14th century but completed by Vasari in 1589. In the area comprised by these palaces are some ancient **Tower-Houses** of the 13th century.

Left: *Tabernacle with the Four Crowned Saints, by Nanni di Banco.*

CHURCH OF SAN LORENZO

A few steps away from the religious centre of the city is the **San Lorenzo Quarter**, with its picturesque open-air market. In the area comprised by the Piazza and the Via Cavour is the **Palazzo Medici**, built by **Michelozzo** in 1444, and one of the most typical examples of Florentine Renaissance architecture. This was the residence of Cosimo the Elder, Piero, Lorenzo the Magnificent and all their court of writers and artists. Particularly noteworthy inside the palace are the **Baroque Gallery** and the **Chapel** with frescoes of the Journey of the Magi by Benozzo Gozzoli. The centre of the area is dominated by the monumental complex of the Church of San Lorenzo, the church that Cosimo Medici the Elder had erected to replace the ancient chapel of San Ambrogio (393), and that he wished to have close to his palace as the parish church. The basilica we see today is a magnificent Renaissance creation of **Brunelleschi** (1419). Michelangelo, as part of his design for the external façade (which was never built), added the inner rear wall. He also built the famous **Biblioteca Laurenziana** in the cloisters adjoining the church, with its wonderful stairway in the vestibule. Internally, the church has a Latincross plan. In front of the high altar is a commemorative stone indicating the spot where **Cosimo the Elder** lies buried. At the end of the nave are the two bronze pulpits sculpted by Donatello, while in the left transept is the **Old Sacristy**, a youthful work of Brunelleschi with the tomb of Giovanni and Piero, sons of Cosimo the Elder. Incorporated in the right transept is the **New Sacristy** designed by **Michelangelo**; it now forms part of the Museum of the Medici Chapels.

Overall view of the Basilica with the picturesque market of San Lorenzo.

MEDICI CHAPELS

The entrance is located in the adjacent Piazza della Madonna. In, the huge **Medici Crypt**, which we see immediately after the entrance hall, are buried almost all the Medici. From here we enter the sumptuous octagonal **Chapel of the Princes**, designed by Matteo Nigetti and commissioned by Grand-Duke Ferdinand I to glorify his family. The gilded statues in the niches above the sarcophagus are of Ferdinand I and Cosimo II. A short corridor leads into the famous **New Sacristy**, commissioned by Giulio de' Medici, later Pope Clement VII. in 1520. It is one of Michelangelo' s greatest masterpieces.

Its theme is that of man faced by eternity, represented by the reclining statues over the two sarcophagi personifying Day and Night, Dawn and Dusk. Above the sarcophagi are the statues of Giuliano, Duke of Nemours, and Lorenzo, Duke of Urbino. On the entrance wall can be seen the incomplete **Tomb** of Lorenzo the Magnificent and his brother Giuliano. At the centre is Michelangelo's youthful sculpture of the Virgin and Child; the two Saints at its side are the work of his pupils. In the apse of the New Sacristy and in an adjacent room were recently discovered, on the walls, a series of 56 drawings attributed to **Michelangelo**; they have now been restored and are on show.

The Medicean Chapels.

Right-hand page: *Partial view of the interior of the New Sacristy.*

20

THE CHURCH AND CONVENT OF SAN MARCO

Halfway down the Via Cavour, on the right, the large Piazza San Marco opens up. Here stand the **Church** and **Convent of San Marco**. The property of the Sylvestrine monks since the 13th century, the Convent was ceded to the Dominicans of Fiesole in 1436. The whole complex was then reconstructed by Cosimo the Elder under the direction of Michelozzo. Illustrious personages such as **Gerolamo Savonarola** and **Fra Angelico** lived in the Convent. Suppressed in 1866, the Convent was turned into a Museum.

Dedicated to Fra Angelico, it contains almost a hundred of his works. Particularly suggestive are the **Cloister of Sant'Antonino** and the numerous little cells of the Dominicans, which retain their ancient structure and the frescoes of Angelico that adorn their walls. Among the more celebrated of his paintings on show we may mention the Last Judgement, the Tabernacle of the Linaioli (commissioned by the guild of linenworkers: 1433), the Deposition (1435) and the Annunciation. In the small Refectory is Ghirlandaio's painting of the Last Supper.

Beato Angelico - Deposition.

PIAZZA AND CHURCH OF THE SANTISSIMA ANNUNZIATA

Just a few minutes walk from San Marco, by way of the Via Battisti, we come to the Piazza dell'Annunziata. The piazza, one of the finest in Florence, is surrounded by porticoes on three sides: the porticoes respectively of the **Church of the Santissima Annunziata** at the far side of the piazza, that of the **Confraternity of the Servants of Mary** on the left side, and the more famous portico of the **Ospedale degli Innocenti** on the right.

Designed by Brunelleschi, it served as a foundlings' hospital. Its portico, consisting of nine arcades, is decorated by **Andrea della Robbia's** ten glazed terracotta medallions of infants in swaddling clothes.

Left: *Equestrian statue of Ferdinando I, by Giambologna.*
Below: *Church of the Santissima Annunziata: portico on the façade.*

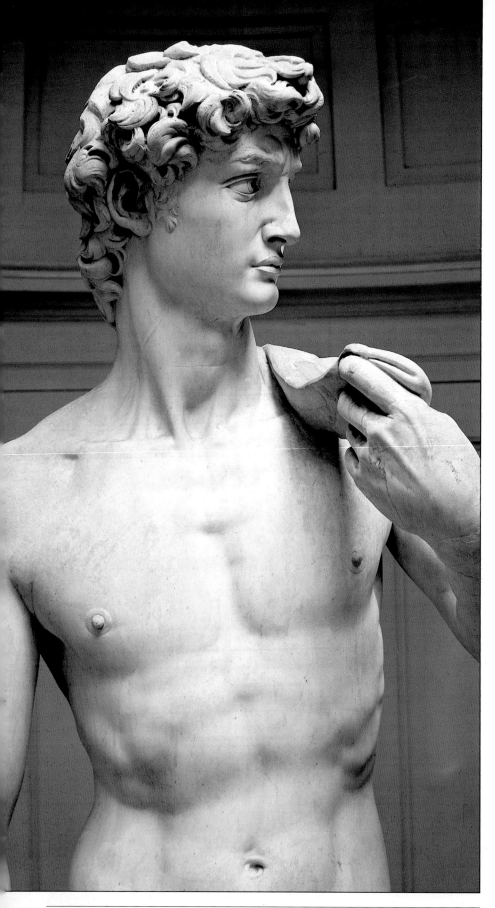

Above: *Michelangelo's David (detail)*.
Right-hand page: *The David, in the Gallery of the Accademia*.

THE ACCADEMIA

Founded by Grand-Duke Pietro Leopoldo in 1784, the Accademia was enlarged and reorganized in the last century. In 1873 the architect **Emilio de Fabris** built the Tribune specially to house Michelangelo's huge statue of David. Michelangelo's other works contained in the gallery comprise the four Prisoners, the St. Matthew, and the Palestrina Pietà, which only entered the museum in 1940. The David: it was in 1501 that the Florentine Republic commissioned the statue of David from Michelangelo. The artist was then 26 years old, and it took him some three years to complete this colossus four metres in height. In 1504 the statue was placed in front of the Palazzo Vecchio in the Piazza della Signoria, where it had the role of personifying the freedom won by the city and the determination of the people to defend it. It remained there until 1870. The four famous statues of Prisoners or Slaves remain in their unfinished state, expressing with powerful dramatic force and tremendous plastic tension Michelangelo's conception of the liberation both of the form from the matter and of the spirit from the body. They come from the Grotta del Buontalenti in the Boboli Gardens, where they were placed by Grand-Duke Cosimo I, who received them as a gift after Michelangelo's death. They originally must have formed part of a grandiose project for the Tomb of Pope Julius II, which Michelangelo never succeeded in completing and which was a source of great disappointment and frustration to him. In the gallery we also find a series of magnificent Flemish tapestries of considerable importance and a major picture gallery of works of the Florentine school dating to the 14th, 15th and 16th century. We now retrace our steps to the Piazza del Duomo. Taking the Via del Proconsolo, we come to the Piazza San Firenze, dominated by the baroque façade of the ancient **Philippine Convent** of **San Firenze** (1715), now the **Law Courts**. Facing it is the **Palazzo Gondi**, while to the right rises the handsome bell tower of the **Badia Fiorentina**, the former Benedictine abbey dating back to the 11th century. Facing it is the Bargello.

THE BARGELLO

Built in 1255, it was the first public palace of the city. Until 1261 it was the seat of the **Captain of the People**, and later became the Palace of the Podestà, a magistrate elected as representative of the people who was the leading figure in the Republic. The various Podestà who succeeded each other in the course of three centuries are commemorated in the coats of arms still visible on the walls of the courtyard.

In the 16th century, on the fall of the Republic and the establishment of the Medici dukedom, the Duke instituted a special corps to maintain public order in the city. It was headed by the Captain of Justice commonly known as the **Bargello**, whose residence the stronghold became in 1574: hence its name. From 1860 the provisional Government of Tuscany decreed that the building should serve as a **National Museum**.

The Palazzo del Podestà houses the Bargello Museum.

The Bargello, a massive fortress-type building, was built at the side of the medieval tower known as the Torre Volognona.

It is in the shape of a cube and is topped by a Guelf crenellation. The Museum of sculpture housed by the Bargello consists of a suite of large rooms on the ground floor which display works by **Michelangelo** such as his Drunken Bacchus, his tondo of the Madonna and Child whith the Infant St. John the Baptist, his David or Apollo, and his bust of Brutus, works which date between 1499 and 1540. On the first floor are displayed sculptures by **Giambologna** and **Donatello**: his St. George, David and youthful St. John the Baptist, dating to the first half of the 15th century. The second floor is especially dedicated to **Giovanni and Andrea della Robbia** and sculptures by **Verrocchio**, including his famous David in bronze. Other artists represented are Pollaiolo, Rossellino, Benedetto da Maiano, and others. Also of interest is the Arms and Armour Room, and the Medici Collection of Coins and Medals.

Beneath the arcades of the loggia there are bronzes by Giambologna.

CHURCH OF SANTA CROCE

Perhaps the most beautiful gothic church in Italy. Founded in 1295, probably based on designs by Arnolfo di Cambio, and completed in the second half of the 14th century, it is distinguished by its spatial grandeur and the sober, rational clarity of its structural elements. The interior is huge, with a wide nave and two aisles, divided by gothic arches and roofed with exposed beams, in the Franciscan tradition. Santa Croce is one of the major arthistorical treasures of Florence: not only does it contain many masterpieces of painting and sculpture, notably the celebrated **Frescoes of Giotto**, but it is also embellished with the Tombs and memorials of the greatest Italians, from **Dante** to **Michelangelo** to **Vittorio Alfieri**.

The frescoes of Giotto can be admired in two chapels: in the **Cappella Peruzzi** (1320) he painted Scenes from the Lives of St. John the Baptist and St. John the Evangelist, while in the **Cappella Bardi** (1317) he painted Episodes from the Life of St. Francis. In the cloister providing access to the adjoining Convent can be found the **Museum of Santa**

Croce with painting, and sculptures of the Florentine school from the 14th to the 16th century and the famous Crucifix of **Cimabue**, seriously damaged in the floods of 1966. Lastly, to the right of the church, at the far end of a suggestive Cloister, we can visit the **Pazzi Chapel**, one of Brunelleschi's finest works.

In the nearby Piazza Cavalleggeri is the building housing the **Biblioteca Nazionale**, while in the Via dei Benci, at n° 6, is the **Horne Museum**, comprising a fine collection of period furniture, paintings and antiquities.

Also in the environs of Santa Croce, in the Piazza dei Mozzi, is the **Bardini Museum & Corsi Gallery**: another notable collection of furniture, ceramics and arms and armour.

Left: *Santa Croce, Cimabue's Crucifix.*

*Santa Croce -
Bardi Chapel,
stories of
St. Francis:
the Saint
renounces
earthly
possessions.*

PIAZZA DELLA SIGNORIA

It is to medieval town-planners that we owe the existing pattern of the historic city centre of Florence. It has its religious centre in the Piazza del Duomo and the adjacent Piazza San Giovanni, while the centre of its political life is formed by the Piazza della Signoria.

The square is dominated by the **Palazzo Vecchio** with its soaring **Torre D'Arnolfo**, the highest tower in the city, while it is flanked on one side by the broad arcades of the **Loggia dei Lanzi**, or Loggia della Signoria, where the most solemn public ceremonies of Medici Florence were held. Famous statues by Renaissance artists, some substituted by copies to preserve them from erosion and damage, have been placed either in the piazza itself, in front of the Palazzo Vecchio, or in the Loggia, which has thus been turned into a little openair museum. They include Michelangelo's marble David and two sculptures by Donatello, the bronze Judith and Holofernes group and the Florentine heraldic lion known as the Marzocco, alongside the monumental Fountain of Neptune (by Ammannati).

PALAZZO VECCHIO

Massive and foursquare, the Palazzo Vecchio, also known as the Palazzo della Signoria, is situated on a corner of the piazza of the same name.

Its earliest part, whose design is attributed to Arnolfo di Cambio, dates back to the beginning of the 14th century. But construction of the building was protracted for more than two centuries, with a series of additions. Initially built as the seat of the Priori delle Arti (heads of the guilds), the Palazzo Vecchio was subsequently commandeered by Cosimo I as seat of the Medici government.

Palazzo della Signoria, one of the finest examples of fourteenth century civic architecture.

From the entrance we step into the spacious courtyard designed by Michelozzo.

We can then visit a series of impressive Renaissance rooms, including the huge hall known as the **Salone dei Cinquecento** which served as the seat of the Italian government in the last century. Built by Simone del Pollajolo nicknamed **Cronaca** (1495), it is embellished with extensive frescoes by Vasari depicting the major battles of Cosimo I.

The 39 panels in the coffered ceiling represent episodes from the history of Florence and of the Medici: at the centre is the Glory of Cosimo I.

At the foot of the walls are arranged the six sculptural groups of Vincenzo de' Rossi representing the Labours of Hercules and the Genius of Victory by Michelangelo (1534).

A vestibule leads to the **Sala dei Duecento**, built by Giuliano da Maiano in 1477, today the seat of the Town Council.

Interesting too is the Study of Francesco I, decorated by Vasari with portraits of Cosimo I and Eleonora of Toledo by Bronzino. A suite of other rooms follows; they include the **Quarters of Eleonora of Toledo**, the Chapel of Eleonora frescoed by Bronzino and the Chapel of our Lady frescoed by Ridolfo del Ghirlandaio (1514); the **Audience Hall** and the **Sala dei Gigli** (or Lily Room), both the work of Benedetto da Maiano; and the **Chancellery**, which was used as an office by Niccolò Machiavelli, secretary of the Florentine Republic from 1498 to 1512. At its centre stands Verrocchio's beautiful Winged Cupid.

Descending to the Mezzanine floor, we come to the five rooms in which are displayed the collection of paintings and sculptures donated to the city of Florence by the well-known American art historian Charles Loeser in 1928.

The Loggia della Signoria, also known as the Loggia dell'Orcagna.

Left: *Hercules and Diomedes. The sculpture is to be found in the Salone dei Cinquecento, together with many other works: it forms part of the cycle of the Labours of Hercules completely executed by Vincenzo de' Rossi.*
Below: *The Salone (Great Hall) of the Cinquecento: general view.*

THE UFFIZI

On one side of the Piazza della Signoria, a long narrow square opens up between the Palazzo Vecchio and the Loggia dei Lanzi, and extends to the banks of the Arno.

This is the **Piazzale degli Uffizi**. Its typically 16th century scenographic conception we owe to Vasari (1560), who designed for Cosimo I the imposing building that delimits it on three sides. It was intended to house the Offices (Uffizi) of the civic government.

It was Grand Duke Francesco I who deserves the credit for creating the art gallery on the building's upper floor, which he succeeded in wresting from the bureaucracy in 1581.

Francesco gathered together a nucleus of paintings and important sculptures in the Sala della Tribuna, thus initiating a metamorphosis in favour of culture which, thanks to the collecting zeal of his Medici successors as well as of the House of Lorraine, was to turn the Uffizi into the most comprehensive art gallery in Italy and one of the most important in the world. An overhead passageway, the famous **Corridoio Vasariano**, passing over the Ponte Vecchio, joins the Palazzo della Signoria with the Palazzo Pitti, thus establishing a private and direct link between the grandducal residence and the seat of the government.

From 1973 on further accessions to the Uffizi Gallery have been made, including a series of paintings of the 17th and 18th centuries, and the famous **Collection of Self-Portraits** of Italian and foreign artists, grouped by school and nationality. They include those of Vasari, Andrea del Sarto, Raphael and the Carracci among the Italians; and those of Rubens, Rembrandt, Velàsquez, Delacroix right up to Marc Chagall, among the foreign artists.

The entrance hall is hung with two tapestries from the Medici workshop. From here we may enter what remains of the ancient church of San Piero Scheraggi (11th century), demolished to build the Uffizi. Here are displayed the famous cycle of portraits of famous men painted by Andrea Castagno in the mid-15th century and Botticelli's notable fresco of the Coronation of the Virgin dated 1490.

On crossing the **Vestibule**, embellished with frescoes and sculptures, we then climb - if we do not go up by elevator - the 126 steps of the ceremonial stairway that leads to the Print and Drawings Room.

The staircase then continues up to the 2nd Floor, where the entrance to the Galleries is situated.

In this guide we will provide a brief summary of the many masterpieces to be seen in the 44 rooms of this incomparably picture gallery, in which the paintings are hung in chrorological order.

Starting out from the first room, therefore, a complete tour of the

Gallery enables the visitor to follow the development of the various schools and especially the Florentine school from the 13th to the 17th century. The corridors admitting to the various rooms are richly decorated with Flemish and Florentine tapestries of the 16th century and statues and sarcophagi of the Roman period, a large part of them copies of Greek originals.

Room I: contains some pieces of classical sculpture and the high relief of the Seated Wayfarer, a Roman copy of a Hellenistic original. **Room II**: dedicated to the "Tuscan primitives" represented by works of the Luccan, Pisan, Sienese and Florentine school of the 13th century, as well as to Giotto.

The most important of the altarpieces on display are the Madonna in Majesty by Cimabue (1280-85), the Madonna and Childwhith Angels and Saints by Giotto (1305-10) and the Madonna of Duccio di Buoninsegna (1285), which comes from the Rucellai Chapel in Santa Maria Novella.

Room III: is devoted to the Sienese school of the 14th century including an Annunciation by Simone Martini (1333) and works by Ambrogio and Piero Lorenzetti.

Left: *Portraits of the Dukes of Urbino: Federico da Montefeltro - Piero della Francesca.*
Below: *The Birth of Venus - Sandro Botticelli.*

The following rooms are dedicated to the Florentine school of the 14th century and the Tuscan painters of the early 15th century; they include Paolo Uccello's Battle of San Romano, and Piero della Francesca's portraits of Federico di Montefeltro, Duke of Urbino, and his wife Battista Sforza. **ROOM VIII** is dedicated to Filippo Lippi, and **ROOM IX** to Antonio and Pietro Pollaiolo and the youthful works of Sandro Botticelli. In the following 5 rooms, now transformed into a single hall, we find the masterpieces of Botticelli: the Primavera (1447-78), the Birth of Venus, and others.

There follow the rooms devoted to the Umbrian and Tuscan painters of the second half of the 15th century, notably Leonardo da Vinci and his celebrated Adoration of the Magi (1481); then come the Room of the ***Geographic Maps*** and the ***Room of the Hermaphrodite***. **ROOM XVIII** is known as the ***Tribuna***.

It was in this beautiful octagonal room, designed by Bernardo Buontalenti, in 1585, that Francesco I gathered together the select works of art that gave birth to the formation of the Uffizi.

Right: *Portraits of the Dukes of Urbino, Battista Sforza - Piero della Francesca.*
Below: *Spring - Sandro Botticelli.*

Filippo Lippi:
Madonna and
Child.

The room is sumptuously decorated: in the centre is a magnificent Florentine mosaic table, while around it stand a series of wonderful statues of the classical period, notably the famous Medici Venus (3rd century B.C.). The walls are hung with a large quantity of portraits of the Medici, mainly of the Mannerist school. They include Bronzino's wonderful portrait of Eleonora of Toledo. The other rooms are dedicated to Perugino and Luca Signorelli, to Dürer and the Venetian painters of the

This is followed by the room devoted to Titian and Parmigianino. In the subsequent rooms are displayed paintings by Veronese, Tintoretto, Francisco Goya, Rubens and Flemish and Dutch painters. The last room is dedicated to Rembrandt (his Portrait of an old man), Caravaggio, and the Carracci (Baccante). At the end of the corridor is the café and the access to the Terrazza della Loggia, from which a partial panorama of the centre of Florence and of the piazza below can be enjoyed.

15th century, and to the Flemish and German masters of the 16th century. **Room XXV** is devoted to Michelangelo Buonarroti; on display is his celebrated "Tondo Doni" or "Holy Family", painted in 1505 for the wedding of Agnolo Doni and Maddalena Strozzi. In **Room XXVI** we find works by Raphael: his Madonna of the Goldfinch, his Portrait of Leo X, and others. **Room XXVII** contains works of the Tuscan Mannerists, including Andrea del Sarto's Madonna delle Arpie.

The Holy Family - The group is conceived as a single sculptural block, where the masses twist into a spiral and are given movement by counterpoised energies. In the background the fine nudes take on the warmest tones, while the semicircle of wall opens on to a more universalised view. It was painted around 1504, on the occasion of the marriage between Maddalena Strozzi and Agnolo Doni, and for this reason is also known as the "Doni Tondo".

Left-hand page: *Madonna of the Canary - Raphael.*
Above: *The Tribune of the Buontalenti.*

PONTE VECCHIO

This is one of the most famous bridges in the world and the most ancient in the city. In fact it has existed since the 10th century, though its original structure was destroyed by a flood of the Arno in 1333. Reconstructed in stone by Neri di Fioravante in the mid-14th century, it was reserved, by order of Ferdinando I, for the use of goldsmiths alone. Under a central arcade of the bridge, which interrupts the line of jewellery shops, has been placed a bust of **Benvenuto Cellini**, the greatest Florentine goldsmith.

PONTE SANTA TRINITÁ

Destroyed by floodwater on various occasions, it was reconstructed by Bartolomeo Ammannati under the artistic influence of Michelangelo between 1567 and 1569. Destroyed once again during the Second World War (1944), it was rebuilt in exact fidelity to Ammannati's plans, using the same material that had been lost in the Arno. It represents one of the most significant examples of Renaissance architecture, combining as it does functionalism of purpose, solidity of structure and elegance of line.

On this page: *The Ponte Vecchio.* Right-hand page: *The Ponte Santa Trinitá (Holy Trinity Bridge).*

PITTI PALACE

In rivalry with the richest families of the city, Luca Pitti, a powerful Florentine banker, jealous of the supremacy of the Medici, commissioned the largest and most monumental of the palaces of Florence from Filippo Brunelleschi in 1440. The original project, of clear classical inspiration, consisted of a groundfloor with three portals and two upper floors pierced by seven windows, each inserted in large arcades.

On the downfall of the Pitti family following an abortive plot against the rulers of the city, the Palace was acquired by Eleonora of Toledo, wife of Grand-Duke Cosimo I. The building was successively enlarged; first by Bartolomeo Ammannati, who opened up two large windows on the groundfloor and built the wonderful courtyard, one of the finest and most significant works of 16th century architecture, because for the first time the courtyard and the palace in which it was placed opened up directly on the gardens behind, achieving a perfect fusion between architectural mass and nature. By a series of later additions by various artists in the 17th and 18th centuries, the Palace attained its present dimensions.

Today the Pitti Palace is the seat of museums and galleries of great importance; they comprise the Palatine Gallery, the Royal Apartments, the Museum of Silverware, the Museum of Historic Coaches and the Gallery of Modern Art.

The entrance façade of the Palazzo Pitti.

PALATINE GALLERY

After the Uffizi, the **Palatine Gallery** is one of the most comprehensive picture galleries in Italy, containing as it does numerous masterpieces of the main schools of Italian and European painting from the 15th to the 18th century. The initiator of the collection that led to the formation of this gallery was Grand-Duke Cosimo II.

During the 17th century the upper parts of the walls and the ceilings of the rooms were decorated in the baroque style by Ciro Ferri and Pietro da Cortona. In 1820 the Gallery was opened to the public by the reigning House of Lorraine and in 1911 was transferred to the State. In contrast to the Uffizi, the rich collection of paintings in the Palatine Gallery is not displayed in chronological order. On the other hand, it would hardly have been appropriate to follow strict museological criteria in a suite of apartments in which everything recalls the sumptuousness of the royal residence it formerly served as. The Gallery is approached by the **Ceremonial Staircase** of the palace, built by Ammannati.

Through the Entrance Hall we reach the **ROOM OF VENUS**, where works by **Titian** are exhibited. In the **ROOM OF APOLLO**, we find further paintings by Titian, as well as of Andrea del Sarto and Van Dyck. In the **ROOM OF MARS** are displayed paintings by Murillo, his Madonna and Child and Madonna of the Rosary, as well as masterpieces by Rubens: his Four

The Sala di Marte. A number of Rubens' most important works are exhibited here.

Above: *The Sala di Giove*.
Right: *The Deposition - by Fra Bartolomeo della Porta. This is among the most beautiful of this artist's works. Note the triangular construction of the group, the red robe of Mary Magdalene in the midst of the softer colours of the Madonna, whose delicate profile is so pure and gentle.*

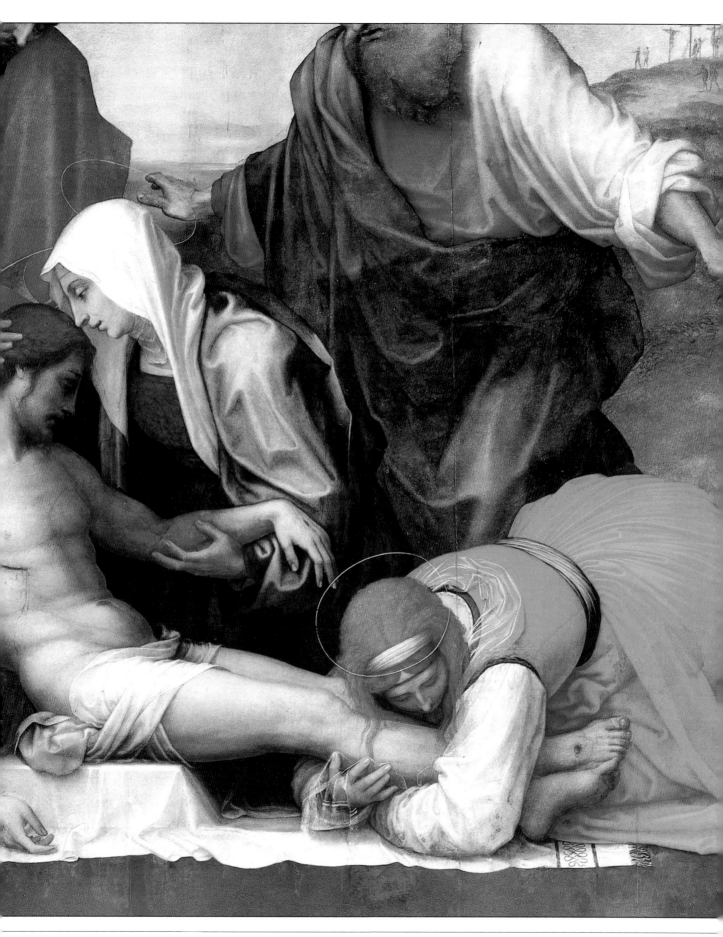

The Sala di Prometeo.
Right-hand page: *Mother and Child and the Stories of Saint Anne,* by Filippo Lippi.

Philosophers and Consequences of War. Other works are also on display: by Guido Reni, Tintoretto and Veronese. **ROOM OF JUPITER**: works by Andrea del Sarto, Rubens again, Bronzino, Raphael (his Veiled Woman) and Perugino (Madonna and Child). In the **ROOM OF SATURN** are collected further paintings by Raphael: his Madonna del Granduca, Madonna della Seggiola and others.

ROOM OF THE ILIAD: here we find yet another painting by Raphael, and works by Andrea del Sarto, Ridolfo del Ghirlandaio, Sustermans, Velasquez and Lorenzo Bartolini. We continue, passing through the Room of the Stove, the **ROOM OF THE EDUCATION OF JUPITER**, the Sala del Bagno, and the *Room of Ulysses*, where Raphael's Madonna dell'Impannata and other works by Tintoretto and Guido Reni are on display. There follow the **ROOM OF PROMETHEUS**, the Rooms of Justice, of Flora and of the Putti, the *Poccetti Gallery*, the *Music Room*, the *Room of the Drums*, the Sala del Castagnoli with its beautiful table known as

"Apollo and the Muses", and lastly the Quarter of the Allegories of Volterrano. In the *Museum of Silverware* (Museo degli Argenti), entered from the left corner of the courtyard, are displayed objects in precious metals and stones and porcelain forming part of the treasures amassed by the Medici and the House of Habsburg Lorraine. *Museum of Carriages* (Museo delle Carrozze): situated in the right wing of the Palace, it contains historic coaches of the 19th and 20th century. The *Gallery of Modern Art;* on the second floor, contains a fine collection of paintings ranging from the **Neoclassical** and **Romantic** periods to the **Macchiaioli** (Italian Impressionists: notably works by Giovanni Fattori) and contemporary Italian art (paintings by De Chirico, Rosai, Marini, Casorati, etc.). The *Royal Apartments* occupy the right part of the first floor with the sumptuous *Throne Room* and the *White Room*, furnished in the neoclassical style and its walls hung with valuable paintings.

The Madonna della Seggiola by Raphael. This painting is believed to have been executed in Rome around 1515-16, and is one of the moust famous works of figurative art. L'erfect intonation bestows a harmony of untouched serenity on the intense vitality of the people portrayed. With her graceful and sympathetic smile, this Madonna seems extremely different from those painted during the artist's Florentino period. The careful calculation of the gestures, the product of a profound equilibrium, mirrors the quiet sweetness of the sentiments, while the hight degree of refinement in her robe,and the use of shimmering colour, shows the influence of Venetian painting. Another admirable feature is the architectural sense which Raphael brings to this ensemble of images. The image of this Madonna, even seen as possessing a touch of the common people, is original and very evocative, as she sits on the chair, holding her little child close to her.

BOBOLI GARDENS

The scenic Boboli Gardens extend over the hill of the same name to the rear of the Palace. They represent one of the greatest, most typical and lavish gardens in the Italian style, laid out over the extensive slopes of a hill between the Pitti palace, the Forte Belvedere and the Porta Romana.

Commissioned by Eleonora of Toledo, the Gardens were begun by Tribolo in 1550, in the very year of the artist's death. They were continued by Ammannati and then, in 1553, by Buontalenti, and completed in the 17th century by other artists including Alfonso Parigi the Younger. The position on the hill, with panoramic views over the city, the rich vegetation, the magnificent fountains, such as that of the Ocean by Giambologna and the Little Bacchus by the entrance, the many statues, all contribute to make the Boboli Gardens a most picturesque public park. At one time they especially served as pleasure grounds for the court and as the scene for the sumptuous festivities of the Medici.

Overlooking the Gardens, on an adjacent hilltop, is the ***Fortess Belvedere***, a splendid example of a military fortress. It was built by Bernardo Buontalento for Grand-Duke Ferdinando I. This unadorned but impressive building is now the venue for art exhibitions and cultural events. The entrance is located on the Viale dei Colli, which we can approach by ascending the picturesque Via San Lorenzo. From the terrace of the Fortress, superb panoramic views over thecity and its environs can be enjoyed.

CHURCH OF SAN MINIATO AL MONTE

The beautiful church of San Miniato occupies a scenic position on the hill of Monte alle Croci, which faces, on the opposite bank of the Arno, the hill on which Fiesole stands. The church was begun in the 11th century and finished two centuries later. It is in the Romanesque style, interpreted in a typically Florentine manner. The polychrome marble facade, with its regular arcading of five arches, dates to the 12th century. In its upper part the geometric taste dissolves: the harmony of the composition is in part lost in the minuteness of the details.

The central mosaic represents Christ Enthroned. Placed over the top of the typanum is the Eagle of the Calimala Guild, Patron of the church. To the right of the basilica we may note the Episcopal Palace, summer residence of the bishops of Florence. On the left stands the ancient Tower in which Michelangelo placed the pieces of artillery for the defence of Florence during its siege by the imperial troops.

The interior of the church is austere but impressive; it emanates a sense of peace, and is embellished with a fine decoration in polychrome marbles, in part falsified by fake-marble revetment.

Especially beautiful is the pavement, inlaid with symbols of the Zodiac and other signs. At the centre of the nave, between the two flights of steps leading up to the choir, is Michelozzo's Chapel of the Crucifix (1448), so called because it was built to house the Crucifix of St. Giovanni Gualberto (now in the church of Santa Trínita).

The raised choir is surrounded by carved marble screens (1207). Also of the same date is the elegant marble pulpit, entirely sculpted and inlaid. The wooden choirstalls are of the 15th century.

The façade and majestic interior, with the Chapel of the Crucifix, by Michelozzo, lit in the centre.

MICHELANGELO ESPLANADE

Just a few minutes walk downhill from San Miniato al Monte brings us to the nearby *Michelangelo Esplanade*. From this panoramic terrace, laid out by the **architect Poggi** in the last century, we can let our gaze rove over the entire Arno valley and the whole of Florence. At the centre of the piazza is the *Monument to Michelangelo*, with a copy of his David and four statues representing Day and Night, Dawn and Dusk.

From one of a number of little streets, or by the Viale dei Colli, we can descend to the city. Continuing along the banks of the Arno (the Lungarno) for a stretch, in a westerly direction, we now enter the popular *Quarter of San Frediano and of Santo Spirito.*

Church of Santo Spirito. It is the most important church of the Oltrarno (the area of Florence south of the Arno). A late work of Brunelleschi (1444), it has undergone various alterations in successive periods. The smooth and simple façade dates to the 18th century.

The interior of the church consists of a Latincross plan with a nave and two aisles divided by Corinthian columns. Here the great art of Brunelleschi, already expressed in the church of San Lorenzo, reached its culmination in the harmony of the proportions and the perfect articulation of the spaces. A series of circular chapels runs round its perimeter. Also of interest are the *Vestibule* designed by Cronaca (1492), the beautiful *Sacristy* built by Giuliano da Sangallo (1489-92), and Orcagna's fresco of the *Descent of the Holy Spirit* (c. 1360). The fine bell-tower was added by Baccio d'Agnolo in 1517.

Also in the San Frediano quarter is the Church of San Frediano in Cestello. The baroque interior is enriched with frescoes by Gabbiani and Curradi. The imposing dome, rising over a cylindrical tambour, is by Ferri (1680- 89).

Between the Palazzo Pitti and the Ponte Vecchio is a church dedicated to the Roman martyr *Santa Felicita*. Vasari's corridor passes over its portico, and opens up on the inside to form a box used by the Grand-Dukes when they attended religious services. The church possesses one of the jewels of Florentine Mannerism: the Deposition painted by **Pontormo** in 1527. Far removed from traditional versions of the subject, without any background and with the figures devoid of corporeality, almost as if suspended in the air, this highly dramatic Deposition is rightly considered Pontormo's masterpiece, not least due to its beautiful iridescent colours.

CHURCH OF THE CARMINE

Begun in a Romanesque-Gothic style in 1268, it was rebuilt after a fire had destroyed a large part of the church in 1771: only the Corsini Chapel and part of the Brancacci Chapel were saved. The 18th century interior has a Latin-cross plan with a single nave. Of exceptional interest is the **Brancacci Chapel**, situated at the end of the right transept. Erected for Felice Brancacci, a rich merchant, man of politics and enemy of the Medici, its walls are decorated with the most important cycle of frescoes of the entire 15th century. They consist of Scenes from the Life of St. Peter, for the most part frescoed with great vigour and solemnity by **Masaccio**, who worked on them from 1425 to 1428. The plasticity of the figures, the individualization and definition of the characters of the personages, and the perfect perspective setting of the scenes, served as a model for all the painters of the Renaissance, including the great Michelangelo himself. The frescoes were begun by **Masolino da Panicale**, continued by **Masaccio**, and completed by **Filippino Lippi**.

Following a superficial cleaning in 1904, which removed

the sedimentations of smoke produced by the 1771 fire, now, thanks to the recent restoration, which has only just been completed, it is possible at last to admire the frescoes restored to the clear and luminous chromaticism of their original appearance.

Left: *The distribution of the alms and the "Death of Ananias" by Masaccio (detail)*.
Above: *The healing of the lame man, and the "Raising of Tabitha" by Masolino (detail)*.

SANTA MARIA NOVELLA

The first monastic church in Florence, it belongs to the Dominicans and dates to 1246, when two friars of the Order, Fra Sisto and Fra Ristoro, began its construction. Leon Battista Alberti added the wonderful green and white marble façade to this medieval church in 1470. The ingenious design of the lateral volutes enhances the harmoniousness of this façade, which is considered one of the most important of the Renaissance. The elegant and spacious interior is in the gothic style, and of great effect is the sense of depth suggested by the rows of pillars which seem to converge as they approach the altar. Of the many works of art in the church we may mention the frescoes by **Ghirlandaio** which entirely cover the walls of the choir behind the high altar. Painted between 1485 and 1490, they charmingly illustrate scenes from the lives of Mary and St. John the Baptist, in a Florentine setting. In the left aisle is **Masaccio**'s fresco of the Trinity, dating to 1427. Adjacent to the church is the Convent. At its entrance is the famous *Chiostro Verde* (Green Cloister), from which access is given to the *Chapter House* or *Spanish Chapel*.

This large rectangular chapel dating to 1350 was allocated by Eleonora of Toledo in the 16th century to the religious functions of the Spaniards in her suite. The vaults and walls were frescoed by Andrea di Buonaiuto in 1355. Especially impressive are the two large frescoes on the lateral walls: they illustrate the Church Militant and the Triumph of the Dominican Order with the Triumph of St. Thomas Aquinas.

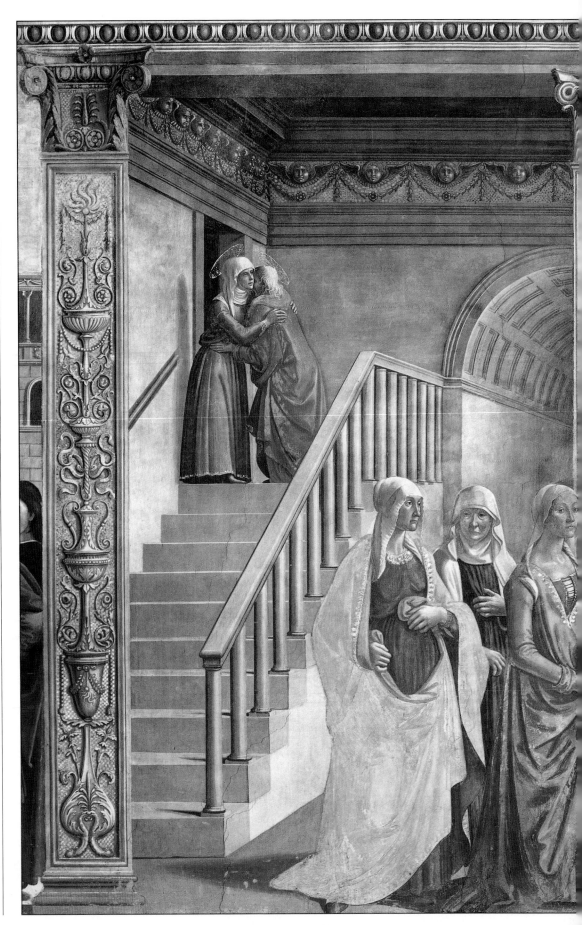

Santa Maria Novella - The Birth of the Virgin by Domenico Ghirlandaio.

NATIVITAS TVA DEI GENITRIX VIRGO GAVDIVM ANNVNTIAVIT VNIVERSO MVNDO x

BIGHORDI

GRILLANDA

PRATO

The handsome city of Prato lies at the centre of the populous plain that extends betwéen Florence and Pistoia. Developed round the ancient parish **church of Santo Stefano**, the present Cathedral, around the turn of the 1st millennium, its historic city centre comprises significant monuments that testify to its past. Yet Prato is also a lively modern town; it is a major centre of the woollen industry. Reports of its flourishing business in the textile field can be traced from the 12th century, by which time the city had already declared itself a free Commune. The industry received a notable boost in the second half of the 14th century, thanks to the involvement of **Francesco Datini**, one of the greatest merchants and bankers of the day. Already by the first half of the 12th century Prato had set itself up as an independent republic. After a series of political and military vicissitudes, it became part of the Florentine Republic in 1351. The Renaissance was for Prato a period of flourishing economic life and artistic and cultural splendour, which was dealt a severe blow by the Spanish sack of the town in 1512. Yet the city succeeded in recovering from thc setback, and went on to enjoy further periods of prosperity and intellectual vitality. In the mid-19th century, while Prato participated actively in the process of Italian unification, the foundations were laid for the economic and demographic expansion that still continues today.

The centre of the town is represented by the Piazza del Comune, dominated by the **Palazzo Pretorio**. This has now been turned into the Civic Picture Gallery (Galleria Comunale), which contains some fine early Florentine paintings. In a small room we find Filippino Lippi's Tabernacle of Santa Margherita (1498), while in the large 14th century salon is Ferdinando Tacca's Fountain of Bacchus. The 2nd floor houses other works includ
ing Bernardo Daddi's Legend of the Holy Girdle and a Madonna by Filippo Lippi. In the room known as the Saletta Verde are displayed baroque works such as Battistello's Noli me Tangere, and in the Saletta Rossa, a series of Views of the Roman Campagna by Kaspar van Wittel.

THE CATHEDRAL

The Cathedral (Duomo), erected at the beginning of the 12th century over the remains of a preexisting church, substantially retains its Romanesque character and Pisan Luccan style. To the right of the 14th century façade is the wonderful **Pulpit of the Sacred Girdle**, designed by Michelozzo and sculpted by Donatello. Over the altar is a Madonna and Child by Giovanni Pisano (1317). From a little courtyard we can enter the Cathe-dralMuseum (Museo dell'Opera) containing numerous paintings, including a fresco of the Blessed Jacopone da Todi attributed to Paolo Uccello. A beautiful little **Cloister** dating to the 12th century also adjoins the church. The Southern and Western Quarters of Prato are full of ancient palaces; they include the **Palazzo Datini** (1330), where Francesco Mario Datini acted as host to sovereigns and famous men. Also in this area of the city are the **Church of San Francesco** and the **Basilica of Santa Maria delle Carceri**. The fortified **Castle of the Emperor**, enclosed behind massive stone walls and merlons of Ghibelline stamp, is also of interest. It was erected by the Emperor Frederick II, following the model of Castel del Monte in Apulia, in the first half of the 13th century. Other little towns and villages in the province of Florence may provide the goal for an agreeable excursion.

Left-hand page: *Prato - The Duomo.*
Right: *Prato - Palazzo Pretorio.*

EMPOLI

An important industrial and trading centre (noted especially for its glassware), Empoli is situated in a fertile plain to the south of Florence, on the left bank of the Arno. The town centre is formed by the **Piazza Farinata degli Uberti**, adorned by Luigi Pampaloni's fine marble fountain with three Naiads and four lions (1827). Looking onto the square to the left is the historic **Palazzo Ghibellino** (1260), while to the right stands the town's main church, the **Collegiata of Sant'Andrea**; adjoining it is an interesting Museum with Renaissance paintings and sculptures.

VINCI

Spread out on a vine- and oliveclad hill not far from Empoli (11 km.), it is especially famous for having given birth to its most illustrious citizen, **Leonardo**, on 15 April 1452. The date is marked each year in Vinci by cultural events in his hon-our. The **Castle**, situated in the upper part of the town, houses the **Vincian Museum**, which contains many models of machines designed by Leonardo. On the 1st floor is a research library, the **Biblioteca Leonardiana**.

CERTALDO

A few kilometres south of Empoli, after Castelfiorentino with its handsome treelined piazza and ancient church of Santa Verdiana, we come to Certaldo, at the centre of the Val d'Elsa. This town too, whose upper part retains its essentially medieval aspect, is famous for having given birth to another famous man: **Giovanni Boccaccio**, author of the Decame-ron (born 1313). The House of Boccaccio, a medieval brick building with a sturdy tower and loggia, is situated on the street of the same name, which begins opposite the fine **PalazzoPretorio**, seat of the Counts of Alberti till the 13th century, then of the Podestà, and then of the Florentine Vicars. The building, its façade adorned with the enamelled ter-racotta and stone coats of arms of the Vicars, is a 15th century reconstruction. Inside we may visit the tribunal (**Camera delle Sentenze**) with fine frescoes; the **Audience Hall** with a frescoed Pietà of the school of Fra Angelico; the beautiful Renaissance courtyard and the **Chapel of San Tommaso** with remains of frescoes by Benozzo Gozzoli. After visiting other rooms on the 1st floor (**Sala Grande** and **Sala del Consiglio**), we may ascend the tower, which commands fine views over part of the ancient and modern town and the picturesque surrounding countryside.

PISTOIA

Situated at the foot of the superb backdrop of the Appennines, Pistoia, a lively old Tuscan town, is still expanding: its more recent developments extend towards the plain and the green foothills.

The most ancient part of the town is enclosed within the extensive quadrilateral formed by the Medici ramparts. Ancient Pistoia, dating back perhaps to the 2nd century B.C., is testified by archaeological remains found in the town, and it was cited by Sallust as the scene of Catiline's defeat in 62 B.C.

Later, in the Middle Agea, it became a free republic on the Ghibelline side and, in spite of struggles against Lucca, Florence, Prato and the Conti Guida, rose to prosperity in agriculture, industry and trade. It was during the 13th century that Pistoia enjoyed the most fruitful period in its history and in its art; it was then that the city, still unsubdued by to the threats and the attacks of its rivals Florence and Lucca, enjoyed a fortunate period of prosperity with trading and banking activities spreading throughout Europe. In the following century Pistoia succumbed to Florentine domination.

The rule of the Medici Grand-Dukes was followed, in 1737, by that of the House of Lorraine with concomitant economic advantages.

After the brief French occupation until 1859, the city became part of the new Italian state.

The medieval town centre is represented by the magnificent **Piazza del Duomo**, which is dominated by the tall bell-tower flanking the Romanesque Cathedral.

Facing it on the other side of the square is the graceful jewel of the **Baptistery**, while on the other two sides of the piazza stand the rectangular gothic edifices of the **Palazzo Pretorio** and the **Palazzo del Comune** founded in 1294 and

enlarged during the 14th century; characteristic is the overhead corridor that links it with the Cathedral, added in the first half of the 17th century. These and other monuments, together with the wonderful works of painting and sculpture they contain, make Pistoia a small but fascinating city of art.

THE CATHEDRAL (DUOMO)

Its construction, together with the massive bell-tower by which it is flanked (67 m. in height), dates to the 12th-13th century. Its façade, with three rows of galleries, is richly decorated with enamelled terracottas, including Andrea della Robbia's Madonna and Child between two angels over the door.

The simple interior with a nave and two aisles contains the Tomb of Cino da Pistoia, a Sienese work of the 14th century. In the **Chapel of San Jacopo** is the famous **Silver Altar of St. James**, a masterpiece of the silversmith's art (13th-14th century); illustrating scenes from the Old and New Testament, it is thronged with 628 figures, with St. James enthroned above. From the Sacristy we may enter the **Chapter Museum** with the Treasury of the Cathedral. Facing the Cathedral is the octagonal gothic Baptistery of the 14th century.

It was built by Cellino di Nese after a design by Andrea Pisano. To the right of the Baptistery is the Palazzo del Podestà (or Palazzo Pretorio), an austere building of 1367. Enclosing the piazza on the opposite side is the Palazzo Comunale, a sandstone building begun in 1294 and completed by the Sienese Michele di Memmo in 1385. It consists of a groundfloor portico of five gothic arcades with upper storeys pierced by elegant two- and three-light mullioned windows.

Behind it lies the medieval **Ospedale del Ceppo**, a hospital still in use; it derives its name from the hollow tree-stump ("ceppo") where alms were deposited. Its façade has a graceful portico decorated with a fine terracotta frieze by the Della Robbia family. Just a few steps away is the little **Church of Santa Maria delle Grazie**, designed by Michelozzo. By way of the Via Buonfanti we may reach the 12th century **church of San Bartolomeo in Pantano**, Pistoia's oldest church; its interior, with tall and narrow nave and side aisles, is notable for its fine Pulpit carved by Guido da Como (1250).

It is supported on three columns: two resting on lions and the third on a bending man.

Also of interest is a visit to the **Church of Sant'Andrea** which contains the famous Pulpit of Giovanni Pisano, one of the masterpieces of Italian sculpture.

Other churches not far from the city centre include **San Giovanni Fuoricivitas**, once outside the walls, with a finr Pulpit by Fra Guglielmo di Pisa, a follower of Nicola Pisano, and the Visitation, a superb high relief by the Della Robbia family.

Left-hand page, above: *The Baptistery.*
Below: *The Town Hall.*
On this page: *The façade of the Duomo.*

The Church of the Madonna dell'Umiltà contains eight 18th century frescoes by es Giuseppe Gricci. Nearby is the **Diocesan Museum** in which import ant works of art from churches in Pistoia and its environs are on display.

Also worth visiting is the **church of San Francesco**, begun in 1294 and finished in the 15th century; apart from fragments of frescoes of the 14th century, it has a beautiful late 14th century **Chapter House** with two fine mullioned windows and interesting capitals. The adjoining convent is also of interest, with cells decorated in the 17th century.

Above: *The façade of San Bartolomeo in Pantano.*
Right-hand page: *The interior of the Church of Sant'Andrea, with the Pergamo by Giovanni Pisano.*

MONTECATINI TERME

Montecatini Terme, "the queen of waters", one of the most renowned spas in Italy, is situated between Pistoia and Lucca; it lies in the plain of the scenic Valdinievole, which the peaks of the Appennines protect from the cold winds of the north. The curative properties of Montecatini's waters were already recognised as early as the 14th century, but their systematic exploitation, though instigated by the House of Lorraine who built the "Tettuccio" thermal establishment, really dates to the last century. Today, a wideranging complex of elegant and wellequipped establishments, in which the health properties of the saline-sulphurated-alcaline waters are exploited according to the most modern criteria, is distrib-

uted over an extensive area of parkland. Montecatini is thus essentially a modern and lively resort town: one of those fortunate localities in which the picturesque landscape and the riches of the earth have been exploited and enhanced to make a stay there agreeable and restful.

Apart from the "*Tettuccio*" establishment, which is the most important, other thermal springs are active at Montecatini, such as the *Tamerici*, *Torretta*, *Regina*, *Rinfresco*, *Giulia* and *Leopoldina*, whose warm saline waters are especially used for the treatment of liver disorders and digestive troubles.

A visit to Montecatini Alto is of interest; its monuments include the stone medieval "*Ugolino*" *Tower*, the remains of the ancient Castle, and the *Church of San Pietro* with a Romanesque bell-tower. From on top of the hill on which the picturesque little town stands, fine panoramic views can be enjoyed over the spa below, the *Val di Nievole* and the encircling wooded foothills of the Appennines.

Left-hand page,
above:
*The "Tettuccio"
warm springs
spa.*
Below:
*Entrance to the
"Tettuccio".*

On this page:
*Park of the
Springs.
Monument to
the Fallen.*

LUCCA

If seen from the air, the city of Lucca looks like an island in the fertile plain, surrounded by a green circle of trees: this is the wonderful tree-lined promenade laid out by the architect Lorenzo Nottolini on top of the massive 16th century ramparts that have for centuries defended the city's independence.

In origin a Ligurian settlement on the frontiers of Etruria, Lucca became a Latin colony in 180 B.C. and a "municipium" in 89 B.C.; it was in this period, and in the 2nd century A.D., that it enjoyed its greatest prosperity, as testified by the remains of its amphitheatre, its first circuit of walls, theatre, and Baths of Massaciuccoli. In the Dark Ages Lucca had considerable importance as a staging post and military centre. It is easy enough to identify the structure of the ancient Roman "municipium", with its gridiron of streets, in the plan of the city, over which was grafted the complicated network of medieval constructions. In the course of the 12th and 13th centuries, which marked the highpoint of the prosperity and power of Lucca in the Middle Ages, a great deal of building took place. The main religious monuments of the city arose, such as the Cathedral of San Martino, San Giovanni, San Michele in Foro and San Frediano. Of the numerous towers that, as a symbol of prestige, rose over the houses of Lucca, only a very few remain today, including the Torre delle Ore: for the most part they were truncated, and later demolished, as a result of the civil strife that agitated the political life of the town.

By the end of the Middle Ages Lucca had assumed a well-defined character, to which the following centuries made no very appreciable changes. During the 15th and 16th centuries various monumental palaces, especially inspired by the models of the Florentine Renaissance, were added. Apart from the Palazzo Pretorio, we may mention the Palazzo Ducale which was for centuries, and indeed still is, the centre of civic political life.

The spacious tree-lined **Piazza Napoleone** or **Piazza Grande** forms the town centre. On its west side stands the **Palazzo Ducale** (now Palazzo della Provincia). It was begun by Ammannati in 1578 and completed in 1728 by Francesco Pini with the addition of the right wing. The interior of the building was largely the work of the architect Nottolini: his grand staircase leading up to the **Biblioteca Nazionale** is striking. A short distance from the piazza is the **Church of San Giovanni**, comprised of two buildings: the **Church of Santa Reparata** and the **Baptistery** dedicated to San Giovanni (14th century). Just after the church we enter the Piazza San Martino, dominated by the marble-clad Cathedral with its massive battlemented bell tower.

THE CATHEDRAL

The Cathedral (Duomo), on which the influence of the Cathedral of Pisa and the typical motifs of the Lombard Romanesque style is apparent, represents one of the most splendid examples of medieval Italian architecture. The original nucleus of the church, dedicated to **St. Martin**, was founded by St. Frigidian (or Frediano) in the 6th century. Seat of a bishopric from the 8th century, the Cathedral was rebuilt and enlarged in 1070, but it assumed its present appearance between the second half of the 12th century and the end of the 15th century. The façade, whose asymmetry is determined by the pre-existing bell tower, was completed by Guidetto da Como in 1204, and is the sole Romanesque part. The interior was entirely remodelled in the gothic style from 1372; its nave and two aisles are divided by slender pillars and topped by cruciform vaults. Numerous works of art preserved inside the church make this jewel of medieval architecture all the more precious. At the centre of the left aisle is the octagonal Tempietto of the Sacred Face, designed by Matteo Civitali (1484); it contains the wooden crucifix (c. 1100) which, according to an ancient legend, was carved by Nicodemus from a cedar of Lebanon and miraculously washed up on the shore at Luni. In the centre of the left transept is the celebrated Sarcophagus of Ilaria del Carretto, second wife of Paolo Guinigi; she died in 1405. The monument, sculpted by Jacopo della Quercia in 1407-08, is reminiscent in its composition of similar French tombs. The Guinigi-Del Carretto coat of arms is carved on one end. Other important works of art can be noted on entering the main door. Immediately to its right is the marble group of St. Martin and the Poor Man. On the third altar of the right aisle is Tintoretto's painting of the Last Supper (1590), while in the Sacristy is Ghirlandaio's fine altarpiece of the Madonna Enthroned With Saints. In the right transept are various works by the local sculptor Matteo Civitali, such as the two wonderful Angels in the Chapel of the Sacrament. In the left transept, just next to the choir, is the Altar of Liberty, sculpted by Giambologna in

1577; the statue of the Risen Christ is by the same artist. The statue of St. John the Evangelist close to the altar is by Jacopo della Quercia. In the same piazza is the building housing the Cathedral Treasury (Opera del Duomo), containing some fine works of medieval silversmith's work. Behind the apse of the Cathedral, after passing the Bishop's Palace, we reach the **Oratory of Santa Maria della Rosa**, a guild church built in 1309. By the Via della Rosa we then reach the **church of Santa Maria Forisportam**, built outside the Roman walls. The interior has a nave and two aisles divided by columns. On the high altar is a shrine by Vincenzo Civitali containing a beautiful statue of the Virgin (17th century). The granite Roman column set up in the middle of the piazza marked the finishing post of the Palio (horse race) run on the occasion of feast days right up to the 18th century. Turning into the Via Santa Croce we come to the ancient **Gate of Saints Gervasio and Protasio**, a survival of the circuit of walls of 1260. This stretch of the walls is now followed by the **Via dei Fossi**, a characteristic street with a canal at its centre which divides the eastern part of the town. Close by, in the Via Guinigi, we

Above:
Particular of the paintings by Fra Bartolomeo della Porta, in the Chapel of the Sanctuary.
Below:
A majestic view of the interior of the Duomo.

Right-hand page: *The Madonna enthroned with four saints, by Domenico Ghirlandaio.*

ILARIA'S ETERNAL SLEEP

Ilaria del Carretto, second wife of the Lord of Lucca, Paolo Guinigi, who died very young on 8th December 1405, giving birth to her daughter Ilaria. Some time later, her husband commissioned a funerary monument for her from Jacopo della Quercia, and this was completed in 1408.

Vasari, in the second edition of his "Lives", recounts that the sculptor "in the base of the statue ...introduced several marble cherubs who are carrying a rihand, so lifelike that they seemed to be of flesh and blood; and in the section above the base, he created the image of the wife of the said Paolo, who was buried therein, with the maximum of diligence". He then makes a reference to a detail of the monument:

"In the same stone he also carved a dog in rounded relief, for the faith which she had shown to her husband", indicating that the sculptor wished to symbolise Ilaria's exemplary fidelity as a wife by using the figure of her faithful little dog Diana.

But the gentle Ilaria was not to rest in peace for long. Paolo Guinigi was in fact driven out of Lucca in 1429, and the tomb was dismantled: part of it ended up in the Sacristy, and part in the chapel of the Garbesi, while the stone slab with the cherubs was sent to the Uffizi, and then to the Bargello.

However, we can once again now admire this wonderfull work in its entirety, since it was reassembled and placed in the centre of the transept in 1889, while today it can be seen in the Sacristy. The figure of the reclining woman gives off a calm serenity; despite her immobility, it seems as if she will be waking from one moment to the next, called to life again by the barking of her little dog Diana, stretched at her feet, as if waiting for a signal.

find the **Case dei Guinigi**, a compact nucleus of 14th century houses and towers. The highest of the latter, with ilexes growing on top, rises over the **Palazzo Guinigi**, a brick building of the second half of the 14th century with elegant gothic mullioned windows. Continuing along the Via Sant'Andrea, where the 12th century church of the same name is situated, we come to the **Via Fillungo** (named after an ancient family of Lucca), one of the main axes of the town plan and a lively much-frequented street flanked by ancient town-houses and towers, including the distinctive 13th century **Clock Tower** (Torre dell'Ore), which has rung the hours since 1471. Close to it is the **Church of San Cristoforo**, rebuilt in the 13th century. To the right of its portal are two iron measures with inscriptions of 1296; they were used to fix the measurements of the looms for the weaving of cloth. The church became the seat of the merchants' guild in the same year. Almost at the centre of the Via Fillungo, on the left, the street skirts the **Roman Amphitheatre**, over the ruins of which houses proliferated in picturesque disorder from the Middle Ages on, but which has substantially retained its elliptical plan. The buildings that also occupied its interior were demolished by Lorenzo Nottolini in 1830-39. From the beginning of the Via Fillungo, by taking the Via Busdraghi, we can reach the **church of San Pietro Somaldi** with a façade adorned by three portals of Pisan form. The nearby Via della Quarquonia brings us of the entrance of the **Villa of Paolo Guinigi**, erected by the "lord" of Lucca in 1418. Since 1968 it has been the seat of the **National Museum** of Villa Guinigi: on display are archaeological collections, sculptures from the Middle Ages to the 19th century, paintings, intarsias, period furniture and textiles. The most important works in the museum include Matteo Civitali's Ecce Homo; Pontormo's portrait of Alessandro dei Medici; works by Jacopo della Quercia, Cristoforo Canozzi, Matteo Civitali, and a fine Crucifix by Berlinghiero. We retrace our steps to the Via Fillungo, close to the Amphitheatre, and then turn right into the Piazza San Frediano, where the **church of San Frediano** is situated. According to tradition, the earliest building on the site was erected by Bishop Frediano himself in the 6th century; this churcji named after St. Vincent was of considerable importance from the Early Middle Ages. Like many other churches in Lucca, San Frediano was rebuilt in the 12th century. The last transformation, which conferred on the church its present appearance, involved the opening up of the side chapels, including the **Chapel of the Holy Cross** and the **Baptistery**. Entering the central portal, we see immediately to the right the magnificent **Romanesque Baptismal Font**. Dating to the mid-12th century, it consists of a circular basin with a large inner urn supported by a pillar and topped by an aedicula resting on colonnettes. Sharply characterized is the style of the presumably Lombard master who sculpted in vigorous

Torre Guinigi.

relief the Stories of Moses in four of the six panels that form the external revetment of the basin. At the further end of the church we find fragments of 13th century frescoes and Matteo Civitali's wooden statue of Mary Annunciate (1475). Other works worth noting are Glazed Terracottas by Andrea della Robbia, a Deposition by Pietro Paolini, an Assumption by Masseo Civitali, nephew of Matteo, and in the Trenta Chapel in the left aisle a beautiful Marble Polyptych with statues in niches by Jacopo della Quercia. Near the church is the **Palazzo Controni (now Pfanner)**, built in 1667. Between it and the city walls an elegant 18th century garden is laid out, adorned with many statues and a fountain in which is reflected the handsome façade of the palace. From San Frediano, by continuing along the Via Fillungo, we reach another splendid piaz-

The existing circuit of the town walls of Lucca now consists of a treelined promenade: as we have already mentioned, the ramparts were transformed into an original circular

za in which stands the white marble **Church of San Michele**. It is mentioned with the denomination "ad Foro" or "in Foro" (i.e. the Roman Forum) already in documents of the 8th century, but of the original building only a few fragments remain. The reconstruction, begun in the second half of the 11th century, must have been almost completed by the early decades of the following century. But later in date is the marble blind-arcading revetment of the sides and transepts, also continued along the base of the façade and apse. The interior, of basilica type with a nave and two aisles divided by columns, contains some works of art: Andrea della Robbia's Madonna and Child; Filippino Lippi's Saints Jerome, Sebastian, Roch and Helena; Agostino Marti's Betrothal of the Virgin, and others. On the right of the church stands the **Palazzo Pretorio** (1492), formerly the seat of the **Podestà** (chief magistrate) and his **Tribunal**. In the same piazza, directly facing the church, is the start of the Via del Poggio, on which is situated the house in which **Giacomo Puccini** was born. Just a few steps further on, by the Via Galli Tassi, we come to the **Palazzo Mansi**, built at the end of the 16th century or beginning of the following century. The sumptuous furnishings of the 17th and 18th centuries have in large part been preserved in its show apartments: one room with Louis XVI furniture; three drawing rooms with walls hung with Brussels tapestries; and the famous **Nuptial Room** (Camera degli Sposi), magnificently decorated with silks, mirrors, stucco-work and intarsias: the alcove containing the canopied bed is separated from the rest of the room by an ornate baroque arch in gilt wood, supported by caryatids. Now the property of the State, the palace houses the **Pinacoteca Nazionale** (Picture Gallery). Among the pictures of considerable value we may mention Pontormo's Portrait of a Youth and Domenico Beccafumi's Continence of Scipio.

Above: The white façade of the Church of San Frediano. Right: Interior of Church of San Frediano.

promenade by Marie Louise of Bourbon at the beginning of the last century.

Built between 1504 and 1645, the walls constitute an interesting example of Renais-sance military engineering. They are in fact Lucca's third circuit of walls. Over four kilometres in circumference, they are formed of **Twelve Curtains** and **Eleven Bulwarks**, with an external height of 12 metres and a thickness at the base of 30. If we walk right round the city on top of the ramparts, we will pass the various **Gates** leading into the city and enjoy panoramic views over it from every side.

Above:
*The Church of
San Michele in
Foro.*

Left:
*An external
view of the city
walls.*

THE VILLAS OF LUCCA

After the palaces, the churches, the museums full of masterpieces of art, it is appropriate that we should complete our itinerary of Lucca by indicating some of the main sights in its environs. These may be the goal of a number of agreeable and interesting excursions in the verdant hills that surround the city. We should point out, first and foremost, the splendid villas situated just a few kilometres to the north of Lucca.

Prominent among these, due to the magnificence of their parks and the refmed elegance of their architecture, are the Villa Mansi near Segromigno, and the nearby Villa Torrigiani, both open to the public. The **Villa Torrigiani** at **Camigliani** dates to the second half of the 16th century, but was enlarged and its front completely transformed by Alfonso Torrigiani in the first decade of the 18th century. Placed at the end of an avenue 700 metres long flanked by two rows of very high cypresses, the great portal leading into the garden is superb and ornate. Inside the Villa, the unusual ellipticalplan staircases and the lavish decoration of the central salon also date to the early years of the 18th century. Built in the second half of the 16th century, the **Villa Mansi** was enlarged, and its façade remodelled, by Muzio Oddi in c. 1635. In the followmg century the Abbé Gian Francesco Giusti made further alterations to the façade. The large 16th century garden was also subjected to major alterations in the following three centuries.

At the locality of Fraga, also to the north of Lucca, is situated the **Villa Marlia**, a former imperial villa, restored and embellished by Elisa Bonaparte Baciocchi.

It is surrounded by a huge park and also equipped with an astronomical observatory. Many illustrious guests stayed here, including Niccolò Paganini and the Austrian Secretary of State Metternich.

Above: *Villa Reale di Marlia.*
Below: *Villa Mansi.*

Villa Torrigiani.

THE VERSILIA

The seaboard district of Versilia is the northernmost extension of Tuscany facing onto the Tyrrhenian, to which the jagged and snow-capped peaks of the Apuan Alps form an incomparable backdrop. At the foot of this short Alpine range, which presents all the majesty of true alpine scenery, the gently rolling hills of the Versilia, clad with woodland, vineyards, olive groves and cypresses, descend to the fertile plain. The intense azure of the sea and the dark green of the thick pinewoods are the dominant notes of the wide crescent of the Versilian littoral; this stretch of beach, from Viareggio to Marina di Carrara, uniform in expanse and dense with bathing establishments, constitutes one of the main tourist centres of the Tyrrhenian coast.

VIAREGGIO

Viareggio, modern and elegant, is spread out between two extensive pinewoods, and preserves, in many buildings and in the structure of some of its districts, a style similar to the belle-époque. The centre of town life is formed by the long treelined avenue that runs parallel to the coast from the port canal, flanked by numerous hotels, villas and shops. Apart from its excellent resort facilities, numerous showbusiness and cultural events make Viareggio a holiday centre of international fame: the most important of these events are the famous **Carnival** and the **Viareggio Prize** for Literature.
Towards the west, as if forming a single urban area, lies **Lido di Camaiore** with its beautiful parish church of the 13th century. It is followed by **Pietrasanta**, founded by Guiscardo Pietrasanta, podestà of Lucca, in 1254. Its town centre is of considerable urbanistic and artistic interest. Its monuments include the **Cathedral** (1256-58), the **Baptistery** and the

Palazzo Pretorio, former seat of the Captains of Justice. The Italian poet **Giosuè Carducci** was born nearby, at **Valdicastello**. Continuing northwards we next come to **Forte dei Marmi**: its name derives from the Fortress, still existing, built by Leopoldo I in 1588, around which the town developed. The pier, stretching out to sea for some 300 metres, not only provides panoramic views of the shoreline and the Apuan Alps beyond, but also serves as a landing stage for the steamers and pleasure boats that ply the coast, from Viareggio to the Tuscan Archipelago and the neighbouring resorts of Porto Venere and Lerici.

The fame of Viareggio is inseparably linked with its **Carnival**, whose elaborate floats and fancydress parades have for over a century become an eagerly awaited event in the tourist and cultural calendar of the Versilia. Viareggio is also an important fishing town, with a port that can provide landing stages for medium and large-sized vessels; there are also three dry docks for the construction and repair of small-tonnage boats. A beautiful and picturesque treelined avenue, the straight **Viale dei Tigli**, leads from Viareggio to Torre del Lago.

Right: *Viareggio - The Harbour.*

TORRE DEL LAGO PUCCINI

This quiet summer resort, a short distance from the riviera of Versilia and the picturesque Lake of Massaciuccoli, lies on the Via Aurelia, between Pisa and Viareggio, not far from Lucca.

Of interest is a visit to the House of **Giacomo Puccini**, which retains its original furniture and numerous mementos of the composer (1858-1924), who composed most of his operas here. His tomb, sculpted by Antonio Maraini, is housed in a room, transformed into a chapel.

And a fine bronze statue of Giacomo Puccini can be seen in front of the house, at the centre of the garden facing the lake.

Tower of Lake Puccini - The Lake of Massaciuccoli.

MASSA

Situated at the foot of the soaring Apuan peaks, not far from the sea, Massa is an important marble-quarrying centre. Its oldest part, fortified and occupying an enchanting position on a hilltop dominating the coast, dates back to the early years of the 11th century. A typical medieval fortified town, with narrow winding alleyways, it comprises the 16th century **Palazzo Malaspina** (seat of the lords of the town). At the foot of the old town, in the plain below, is the new town, begun in the 16th century and rapidly expanded in recent years. A few kilometres from the town, on the coast, is Marina di Massa, a pleasant and popular seaside resort spread out amid pinewoods. The town centre of Massa itself is formed by the airy **Piazza degli Aranci**, which takes its name from the double row of orange trees that surround it on three sides. The fourth side is occupied by the imposing facade of the **Palazzo Cybo Malaspina**, completed at the beginning of the 18th century. The **Cathedral**, also at the centre of the town, was enlarged by the Malaspina in 1447. It has a baroque interior, to the right of which is the **Baptistery**; steps lead down from it to the funerary chapel of the Cybo Malaspina family and of the Bishops. In the upper part of the old town is the medieval **Fortress** (Rocca), where the Malaspina constructed this elegant palace in the Renaissance style between the 15th and 16th century. It is crowned by a beautiful loggia supported on twinned colonnettes. Massive bastions encicle the fortress, and from the ramparts magnificent panoramic views can be enjoy ed towards the sea and over the Apuan Alps behind.

CARRARA

Not far from Massa lies the city of marble *par excellence:* Carrara. This is a modern town, but embellished with interesting monuments, among them the **Cathedral**, Romanesque in structure, Gothic in decoration. Begun in the 11th century, it was completed in the 14th. **Marble** is the real inexhaustible resource of the Apuan region; it is considered the most important deposit in the world. From these quarries, which have been exploited since antiquity, are extracted a number of different varieties of marble, from the precious white Carrara used in statues to the ordinary white and the speckled Bardiglio.

Marble-quarrying activity in Versilia was modest until the advent of Michelangelo Buonarroti. A further increase was registered with the arrival of new mechanical quarrying techniques in the last century. The great blocks of raw marble are transported from the quarries to the port of Marina di Carrara by a scenic railway, itself a daring feat of engineering. Marina di Carrara, at the northernmost point of the Tyrrhenian coast of Tuscany, is a pleasant seaside resort and centre for the shipment and export of marble. At the beginning of the Via XX Settembre are the modern pavilions of the **National Exhibition of Marble**, where the various aspects of the excavation, transport and working of marble are displayed. Also on show is the famous **Roman Shrine** found in one of the quarries with mythological figures of Jupiter between Hercules and Bacchus.

The marble quarries.

PISA

One of the most interesting and most visited cities in Tuscany is Pisa, due to its many monuments that testify to the splendour reached by the ancient Maritime Republic. In the course of the epic conflict between the Christian and Islamic worlds represented by the Crusades, Pisa came closse to establishing an empire, opening new maritime trade routes and

founding prosperous colonies on the coasts of the Mediterranean. And it was at sea, in the tragic naval battle of MeIoria, that the fortunes of this city, weakened by intestine strife and by the rivalry of Lucca and Florence on the one hand, Genoa on the other, were ultimately eclipsed. It was in this time span, between the 11th and the 13th century, so fruitful in cultural and economic exchanges, that the major artistic efflorescence of Pisa took place.

The Pisano family of sculptors, assimilating and reelaborating elements of Early Christian art, the Lombard Romanesque and the Arab world, developed a Pisan style and helped to form the wonderful monumental complex of the Piazza dei Miracoli.

Here, on the green lawn, rests the massive yet graceful stone cylinder of the Baptistery, facing the magnificent Cathedral. The motif of the open galleries of its façade is echoed in that of the tiered galleries of the Leaning Tower. The beautiful Camposanto extends along one side of the piazza, a place of peace and meditation, and a worthy completion of this wonderfully organic monumental complex unique in the world.

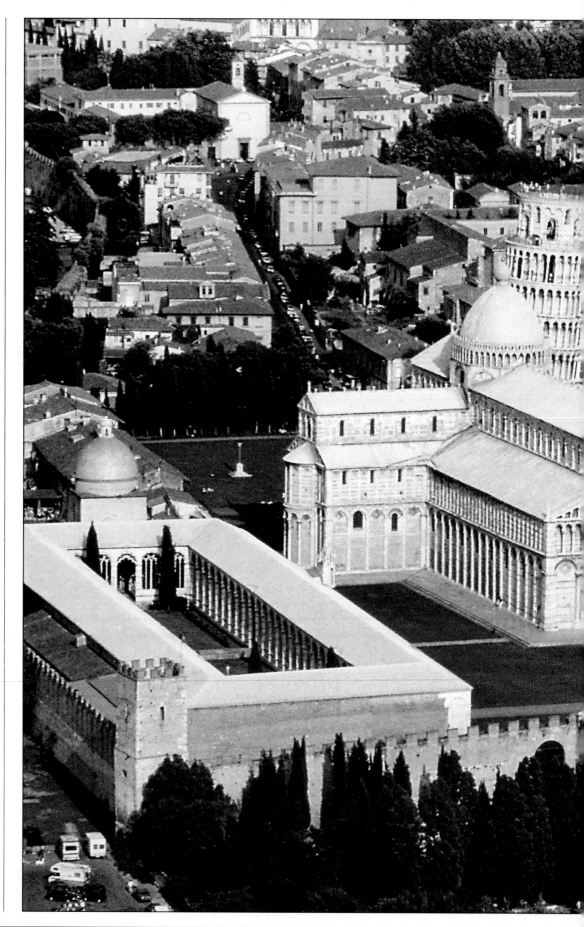

Piazza dei Miracoli, aerial view.

THE CATHEDRAL

It arose in the most fortunate period of the political and mercantile expansion of the powerful Maritime Republic: the work was initiated in the mid-IIth century under the direction of Buscheto and resumed in the following century by the architect Rainaldo, who enlarged the original plan and completed the wonderful façade where the blindarcading motif of the lower storey is opened out and developed threedimensionally in the graceful arches of the four superimposed open galleries above.

The *interior* is awesome: divided by serried rows of antique granite columns into a nave and four aisles in the longtitudinal body of the church, and two aisles in the transepts. Giovanni Pisano's *Pulpit*, realized by the master in the first decade of the 14th century, is the most precious gem that the Cathedral encloses.

The large bronze lamp hanging outside the choir, at the centre of the nave, was modelled by Battista Lorenzi in 1587; it is also called "*Galileo's Lamp*", because the famous Pisan scientist is supposed to have intuited the principle of the pendulum by watching its oscillations. The large *Mosaic in the Apse* of "Our Lord in Glory" dates to the early 14th century.

The interior of the Cathedral and the Pulpitum by Giovanni Pisano.

THE BAPTISTERY

Its construction extended, with various interruptions, over a long period of time stretching from 1153, the year in which it was begun by the architect Diotisalvi, to the end of the following century. In spite of the fact that its original design was never fully realized, due both to the succession of artists who worked on it and the influence of new architectural styles, the structure of the building does remain substantially Romanesque. Much of the rich sculptural decoration of its

Right-hand page, above: *Interior of the Baptistery with the Font.* Below: *Interior of the Baptistery with the Pulpit.*

upper storeys is attributable to Nicola and Giovanni Pisano; their works, human and animal statues, heads, busts of saints and prophets, have been replaced by rather crude copies to save them from destruction. At the centre of the Baptistery, inside, stands the ***Baptismal Font***, on a podium of three steps. Its severe and essential lines are relieved by the rich polychrome inlays of the panels by which it is surrounded. Conceived for baptism by immersion, a rite more common in antiquity, it consists of a large octagonal basin with four smaller basins inside. Dating to 1246, the Font is the work of Guido Bigarelli from Como. At its centre, a column with an Arabic capital supports the statue of the Baptist by Italo Griselli. The Baptistery's particular acoustic creates a multiple echo effect which is highly suggestive: under the broad cupola, every sound, every song, is polyphonically repeated.

THE PULPIT

Realized by Nicola Pisano in 1260, it is not just a work of sculpture, but also as an architectural element in its own right: in fact, it dissociates itself from the traditional model of the pulpit resting against the wall, and stands isolated on seven columns, some of them resting on lions, and the central column on a plinth sculpted with figures of animals and gnomes. Hexagonal in plan, it is closed on five sides by marble panels sculpted in high relief with Scenes of the Annunciaton and the Nativity, the Adoration of the Magi, the Presentation to the Temple, the Crucifixion and the Last Judgement. Over the capitals, spanned by trilobate arches, are placed personifications of Faith, Charity, Fortitude, Humility, Fidelity and Innocence.

THE LEANING TOWER

The most singular of the monuments in the Piazza dei Miracoli is without doubt the Leaning Tower. It was begun in 1173 by Bonanno, who ingeniously revived the motif of the superimposed galleries of Rainaldo's Cathedral façade. But the construction of the tower, on reaching the third storey, was abandoned because of a subsidence of the soil which caused its characteristic inclination. The work was resumed a century later by Giovanni di Simone, who tried to rectify its lean while simultaneously raising it to its seventh storey. The topmost bell-chamber, of lesser diameter, was added by Tommaso di Andrea Pisano in the mid-14th century.

From the top of the Tower, which is ascended by a spiral staircase, magnificent views can be enjoyed of the gleaming white miracles of art that rise, in such wonderful unity, from the green lawns amid which they stand, and of the city and the surrounding countryside beyond.

THE CAMPOSANTO

The Camposanto (or cemetery), a rectangular funerary enclosure that provides a worthy complement to an architectural complex unique in the world, was built at the close of the 13th century on the spot where, according to tradition, Archbishop Ubaldo del Lanfranchi had deposited shiploads of Earth from Calvary, transported in Pisan vessels on their return from one of the Crusades. Begun by Giovanni di Simone, the building was completed in the following centuries. The large inner walls of the four corridors were frescoed from the second half of the 14th century. Funerary monuments and chapels were erected inside, while numerous Antique Sarcophagi, Classical and Medieval Statues and Sculptures, scattered throughout Pisa, were brought here to embellish the galleries that run round the Camposanto's four sides. The Camposanto thus came to represent a precious artistic heritage, comprising famous paintings and an important museum of classical sculpture, enclosed in a magnificent architectural setting. Today part of these drawings and paintings have been detached from the walls and moved to the **Museum of Sinopias** (preparatory drawings), set up in the ancient Hospital of Santa Chiara, which is also situated in the Piazza dei Miracoli, facing the right side of the Cathedral.

CATHEDRAL MUSEUM

The 14th century building in which the Museum is housed, situated on the eastern edge of the Piazza dei Miracoli, was the seat of the Cathedral's Canons from the 13th century. Acquired by the Cathedral Works, it was, after systematic restoration, recently transformed into a museum.

The works of art on display come from the monumental buildings in the Piazza. The central nucleus of the Museum is on the ground floor, consisting of sculptures ranging in date from the 11th to the 13th century: from the Griffin, a rare Fati mid work, to the polychrome wooden Christ by a Burgundian artist, and an impressive review of the sculptures of Rainaldo and Guglielmo from the Cathedral façade, we pass to the masterpieces of Nicola, Giovanni and Tino di Camaino. To the former two are dedicated three rooms and a side of the cloister; their works include the busts and statues removed from the exterior of the Baptistery, the Madonna del Colloquio and the Madonna of Henry VII. Tino di Camaino, the greatest sculptor of the 14th century, is represented by the Altar-Tomb of St. Ranieri and the group of Hen-

Above:
The Camposanto, western side.

Below:
The Museum of the Opera del Duomo, ground floor.

Right-hand page:
Lungarno Gambacorti - view of the Church of Santa Maria della Spina.

Pages 98:
Piazza dei Cavalieri.

ry VII and his Councilors. The archaeological section might come as something of a surprise in a Museum intended to house objects belonging to the monumental buildings of the Piazza del Duomo. But the antiquities collected here should be read as testimonies to the Etruscan and Roman presence in the territory of Pisa and Volterra, and reused, together with marbles imported from Rome in the Middle Ages, to decorate the buildings of the city, in particular the Cathedral. Apart from the wonderful monuments of the Piazza dei Miracoli, other important works of art and architecture await the visitor with a little time on his hands in Pisa. First, there is the walk along the banks of the Arno: along the **Lungarno Mediceo**, the **Lungarno Galileo** and the **Lungarno Gambacorti**, whence we can admire the view of the tiny but enchanting gothic **Church of Santa Maria della Spina** (1323), a jewel casket in stone topped by a delicate filagree of pinnacles. Its name derives from the fact that it originally contained a relic of a thorn ("spina") from the crown of Christ. Also situated on the Arno is the **National Museum of San Matteo** comprising important sculptures and paintings of the 13th-15th centuries, with works by Ghirlandaio, Masaccio, Giovanni, Andrea and Nino Pisano, Simone Martini, and others. At the centre of the town is the famous Piazza dei Cavalieri, with the fine Palazzo dei Cavalieri that is now the seat of the Scuola Normale Superiore (university college) founded by Napoleon in 1810. It is flanked to its left by the Palazzo dell'Orologio, and to its right by the church of Santo Stefano dei Cavalieri, built by Vasari in 1563-72. It contains trophies and banners conquered from the Turks and the gilt bronze bust of San Rossore, a major work by Donatello (1427). Also in the city centre are a number of important churches enriched with works of art: they include the **churches of Santa Caterina**, **San Zeno**, a medieval jewel of the 10th 13th century, **San Francesco**, **San Frediano** and **San Michele in Borgo**, **San Martino**, the church of the **Holy Sepulchre**, and of **San Paolo a Ripa d'Arno**.
A number of wonderful palaces are also to be seen on the banks of the Arno, such as the 14th century **Palazzo Gambacorti**, now the Town Hall; the **Palazzo Reale**, the **Palazzo Agostini**, **Palazzo Toscanelli**, and **Palazzo dei Medici**. An impressive sight to the west of the city is the **Fortress** or **Cittadella Vecchia**, which with its 13th century Guelph tower is reflected in the waters of the Arno. It was built close to the ancient **Arsenal of the Pisan Navy**. Pisa's traditional festivities are concentrated in the month of June, with the Illuminations of the Lungarni and the Leaning Tower, the Historic Procession, and the Regata of the Ancient Maritime Republics, alternately held each year in Amalfi, Genoa, Pisa and Venice.

VOLTERRA

The Etruscan Felathri, Volterra stands high on a solitary hill, overlooking the surrounding countryside and of the hills that stretch away to the distant backdrop of the Appennines. The hill is precipitous, and the abyss known as the Balze, at the foot of the ruined **Badia**, is awesome; part of the Etruscan walls and the necropolis have been swallowed up by it. Like a stronghold suspended in the sky, Volterra has a commanding presence.

Two colours predominate: the intense blue of the sky and the iron grey of the stone with which the Etruscans built their massive walls and which was used in the Middle Ages to construct the gloomy palaces that still line Volterra's streets. The walls, with the famous round-arched Etruscan gate known as the **Porta dell'Arco**, still encircle the city; the medieval buildings, including the superb **Palazzo dei Priori**, still look onto the piazzas and narrow alleyways.

The town's traditional craft is the working of alabaster, and the workshops of the alabastercarvers add a characteristic note to Volterra.

At the centre of the town is the scenic Piazza dei Priori, one of the finest medieval piazzas in Italy. The historic buildings

Gateway of the Etruscan Arch.

Among the works of art contained in its Latin-cross interior are a *Deposition*, a Romanesque wooden sculpture of the 13th century, and a *Pulpit* sculpted by pupils of Guglielmo Pisano.

Facing the Cathedral is the octagonal self-standing **Baptistery**, built in the 12th century. On the right side of the Cathedral is the **Diocesan Museum of Sacred Art**.

The summit of the hill is dominated by the **Medici Fortress**, a formidable Renaissance stronghold.

The central keep was erected by Lorenzo the Magnificent after 1472.

Also situated in the town centre is the **Etruscan Museum of Volterra**: it contains one of the most interesting Etruscan collections in Italy.

As already mentioned, alabaster has long been worked in Volterra (since 1790); numerous quarries of the stone exist in its territory.

The craft has undergone further growth with the development of tourism, and indeed represents one of the town's main economic resources.

Other smaller towns in the province of Pisa are of interest both for their history and the works of art they contain. **Giuliano Terme**, **Uliveto Terme** and **San Casciano Terme** are three modest, quiet and wellreputed spas.

San Miniato, in the eastern part of the province, has interesting historical and artistic remains. Its **Cathedral** is a magnificent 13th century building; its massive bell-tower was once the tower of an ancient castle.

On the summit of the hill are the remains of the Fortress of Frederick, in which the Countess Matilde was born and in which, two centuries later, Pier delle Vigne was imprisoned and blinded.

by which it is surrounded include the **Palazzo Pretorio**, originally the seat of the Captain of the People. It is faced by the austere 13th century **Palazzo dei Priori**, begun in 1208 and completed in 1254.

Its austere battlemented façade is topped by an elegant bell-tower and relieved by three orders of elegant gothic two-light mullioned windows. The Palazzo dei Priori is now the Town Hall, and also contains, on its second floor, the **Picture Gallery** founded in 1905; it includes works by Florentine, Sienese and Volterran artists of the 14th-17th century, among them works by Rosso Fiorentino, Luca Signorelli, Taddeo di Bartolo and Domenico Ghirlandaio. A few steps away, in the adjacent Piazza San Giovanni, is the **Cathedral** (Duomo), a Pisan Romanesque building of the 13th and 14th century.

Above: *Palazzo Pretorio.*
Right: *The Etruscan Museum.*

LIVORNO

At the southernmost extremity of the Arno's coastal plain, Livorno is Tuscany's second leading city and an important merchant-shipping port. A small village of uncertain origins, "Livorna" is recorded as early as 904. It had a castle in the 11th century, and in 1392 became a fortified port in defence of the Port of Pisa. Subsequently a dependency of the Visconti of Milan and then (in 1405) of Genoa, it was ceded to Florence for the sum of "a hundred thousand gold florins" in 1421. Following the silting up of the ancient port of Pisa, Livorno became, under the rule of the Medici, the most important maritime outlet of the Tuscan State.

During the government of Cosimo I, his sons and Cosimo II, Livorno enjoyed a further development with the construction of the new port, begun in 1571, and the plan of the new town of 1576. After the completion of the Medici Port in 1618, Livorno became a free port, enjoyed further prosperity and by the end of the 18th century had become (with a population of 80,000) Tuscany's second largest city. Today Livorno is a city of modern appearance, a mercantile city

above all, but also popular for the bathing resorts in its vicinity. The port is still very active; it consists of the **Medici Port** and the more extensive **New Port**.

The monument to **Ferdinando I** stands in the large Piazza Giuseppe Micheli; popularly known as the "**Four Moors**", represented by the four bronze statues of "Berbers in chains" sculpted by Pietro Tacca and placed here in 1626. It was from the old harbour of Livorno that **Amerigo Vespucci** and **Giovanni da Verrazzano** left for the New World in respectively 1500 and 1523.

Livorno's **Naval Academy** was founded in 1881 by General Benedetto Brin, who amalgamated the preexisting naval colleges of the Sardinian, Genoese and Neapolitan Navies.

In the centre of Livorno stands the **Cathedral** (duomo), destroyed by bombardments in the Second World

Above: *View of the Medicean Gateway.*
Left: *The Port - The Darsena and the New Fort.*

War, but reconstructed in its original late 16th century form after the war. Dedicated to St. Francis of Assisi, the Cathedral was erected in 1594-1606 after a design by Alessandro Pieroni and enlarged in the 18th century by the addition of chapels. Yet it is the **Fortress**, whose earliest nucleus antedates the year 1000, that represents the major monument of the city: the existing building was commissioned by Cardinal Giulio de' Medici, and erected by the architect Antonio da Sangallo the Younger in 1521-34. At the further end of Livorno extends the bathing area with the "**Pancaldi**" bathing establishment, the oldest of the Livorno seafront.

The winding southern coast of this stretch of the Tyrrhenian littoral is beautiful and varied, characterized by cliffs and little beaches hemmed in by dense pinewoods. At **Antignano** south of Livorno is the crossroads for the **Sanctuary of Montenero**; it derives its origin from an image of Our Lady which, according to legend, was miraculously transported here from the Island of Euboea in 1345. A little further on is the **Castle of Boccale**, which stands on the rocks of the coast and which we see here during a seastorm.

After the daring **Bridge of Calignaia**, we come to **Quercianella**, a quiet and picturesque seaside resort. A little further south, on the edge of the Maremma, lies **Castiglioncello**; laid out round a beautiful beach, this is an elegant holiday centre, scattered among pinewoods that stretch right to the seafront. Continuing southwards along the Via Aurelia, we pass through Rosignano Solvay, Vada and Cecina.

On the left, after the little **octagonal Chapel of San Guido**, we may suddenly glimpse the "**Avenue of Cypresses**" celebrated in a famous ode of Carducci. Leaving the Via Aurelia further to the south, we enter **San Vincenzo**, a seaside resort, and then continue along the popular Maremma littoral to the wonderful **Gulf of Baratti**: it may be admired from on top of the promontory of **Populonia**, an ancient fortified town enclosed within medieval walls. An ancient Etruscan and later Roman port, Baratti was an important centre for the iron ore trade with the Island of Elba.

The Etruscan Necropolis of Populonia developed round its port. The tombs date to the period from the 9th to the 2nd century B.C. and were concealed by the Etruscans with metal slag, coal and the remains of destroyed kilns. Worth visiting in the archaeological area are the **Tomb of the Chariots**, the **Tomb of the Funerary Beds**, and the **Aedicula Tomb**. The rich grave goods found in them are now displayed in the Archaeological Museum of Florence and the **Museum of Populonia**. A few kilometres further south lies **Piombino**, an ancient port of Roman origin, an ironproducing centre of ancient tradition and today an important trading port and embarcation point for the Isle of Elba.

The Medicean Fortress.

THE ISLAND OF ELBA

A mythical aura has long lain over the islands of the Tuscan Archipelago: legend recounts that they were born from the waters when the necklace of Venus broke and the gems fell into the stretch of sea from which the profiles of Elba, Gorgona, Capraia, Pianosa, Montecristo, Cerboli, Palmaiola, Giglio and Giannutri emerge. So much for legend. The real history of Elba and the other islands of the Tuscan Archipelago is not so alluring: it consists of a long series of assaults and invasions, raids and foreign dominations, which have contributed to make this island a law unto itself. The rediscovery of the Tuscan Archipelago, and of Elba in particular, is relatively recent. Up till a few decades ago the Island of Elba was especially a source for iron iron, and a generous producer of excellent wines, which it still is. But tourist activity has been developed to such a point that the island has come to be considered the "*Capri of the North*". It has also gone down in history as the island lived in by **Napoleon**, in exile, after his abdication at Fontainebleau. Many sights on the island devoted to him are associated with Napoleon's stay; and two small but fascinating museums are located in the Villa of San Martino and the Mulini at Portoferraio.

PORTOFERRAIO

Portoferraio, the most important town on the island, is a lively and popular tourist and bathing resort. Its port is the landing-stage for the ferries that ply between Elba and the mainland and connect with the other towns on the island. Its old fortified citadel is worth visiting.

Here, in the Piazza della Repubblica, we find the *Palazzo Comunale* and the *Parish Church* of 1548, and the churches of the *Holy Sacrament and of Misericordia*, in which the death mask of Napoleon is preserved, and two forts: the *Forte Falcone* and the *Forte Stella*.

The former residence of Napoleon, the *Palazzina Napoleonica dei Mulini*, situated between the two forts, is a national monument of considerable historical interest.

Its various rooms furnished with furniture in the Empire Style include the *Study* and *Bedroom of Napoleon* and the *Officers' Mess* with the equestrian portrait of the Emperor by the French painter Jacques-Louis David. The *Napoleonic Villa of San Martino* is 5 km. from Portoferraio. Its rooms furnished with period furniture can be visited. Its *Council Room* (or Room of the Doves) is famous for its "love knot" depicted in the oval ceiling panel: the more the doves, Napoleon and Marie Louise of Austria fly away from each other, the tighter the love knot becomes. Outside Portoferraio, the remains of an important Roman villa can be visited at "*Le Grotte*", it is decorated with mosaics and furnished with a hot water conduit. A little further on is *Bagnaia*, a picturesque fishing village situated in a scenic bay. Driving inland, after passing Volterraio (with a ruined fortress), we come to *Rio nell'Elba* and *Rio Marina*, the two most important settlements on the eastern

Portoferraio - Cala Acquaviva looking towards Capo d'Enfola.

side of the island where once the ironore mines were active.

Not far away is **Porto Azzurro**, dominated by the **Fort of San Giacomo**, now a prison.

From here we may reach Capoliveri, isolated on a hill, a village of very ancient origins.

Its beautiful beach overlooks the **Gulf of Stella**.

To the west, after passing the Gulf of Lacona, with its beautiful beach bordered by pinewoods, we reach **Marina di Campo**.

Its harbour, together with Portoferraio and Porto Azzurro, provides anchorage for the largest number of pleasure boats and fishing boats in the island.

Its beach is also the most extensive on Elba.

Its ancient nucleus is huddled round the Medicean tower, the **Torre della Marina**, on a short promontory. From Marina di Campo we can penetrate inland, ascending to **S. Piero in Campo** and **S. Ilario in Campo**, two charming hill-towns of very ancient origins, far from the sea but popular with holidaymakers thanks to their fresh air and peacefulness. From here starts out the panoramic road of **Monte Perrone**, which crosses the island, before dropping down either to the **Gulf of Procchio** or to **Poggio Terme**, and from there to Marciana, one of the most ancient settlements on Elba.

Marciana Marina, a seafront extension of **Marciana**, is a large fishing centre with an import ant port and a fine beach.

One undemanding and scenic excursion is that up to Monte Capanne, whose cableway departs from between Marciana and Poggio and ascends to 1018 metres: the highest and most panoramic point of the island, commanding views over all its territory.

From Marciana another pleasant walk is to the **Sanctuary of the Madonna del Monte** at an altitude of 750 m.

From here the most beautiful sunsets of Elba can be admired.

It was here, in an adjoining hermitage, that Napoleon stayed from 23 August to 5 September 1814 and met Maria Walewska and her son.

Portoferraio - general view.

Above left:
*Marciana
Marina, a
glimpsed view.*
Above right:
*Porto Azzurro,
general view.*
Below: *Caletta
near Marciana
Marina.*

SIENA

.All the cities of Tuscany, especially those that have best preserved the heritage of their past, have a particular character, a local colour all of their own: Lucca, for example, is essentially Romanesque, Florence decidedly Renaissance. Siena, whose magnificent 14th century urban fabric seems to have been imbued with something of the grace and serenity that animate its surrounding countryside, has an essentially Gothic character.

Two legends are associated with the origins of Siena: according to the first, it was founded by a tribe of Gauls, the **Galli Senones** or **Senes**; according to the second, by **Senus**, son of Remus, hence the Roman shewolf adopted as the heraldic device of the city. After the Roman and Lombard dominations, and the rule of the Bishops, Siena set itself up as a Republic.

The Sienese Republic reached the height of its splendour in the second half of the 13th century and beginning of the 14th, between the victory over the Florentines at Montaperti and the Black Death in 1348. It is to the Government of the Nine, established by the mercantile bourgeoisie in 1287, that the merit is mainly due for having created the monumental grandeur of Siena. It was in this period that the architectural renewal of the city took place, that the magnificent Palazzo Pubblico was raised, and the city embellished with the other public buildings, fountains and gates in the walls that still surround the city. Yet it is in the Piazza del Campo and Piazza del Duomo that the beauty of Siena is epitomized. the pink shell of the Campo suddenly reveals itself to us, like an opening fan, between the houses and palaces, enclosed by the elegant façade of the Palazzo Pubblico, with its soaring Torre del Mangia. On the day of the Palio, moreover, the medieval spirit of this noble city seems to reawaken, in a joyous feast of colours, an uncontainable burst of enthusiasm. In perfect harmony with the Piazza del Campo, the Palazzo Pubblico, with its concave façade, seems to embrace and counterpoint the buildings on the other side of the square. Its construction, begun in 1288, was protracted until 1310. Additions were made later: in 1327 the prisons; in the mid-14th century the Grand Council Hall. The two lateral wings were raised a storey in height: the addition is clearly visible from the hanging arches above the first order of three-light mullioned windows. The palace was formerly the seat of the Podestà (chief magistrate). Today it is the Town Hall

PALAZZO PUBBLICO

INTERIOR: *Sala del Mappamondo*. This large room derives its name from a map of the world painted by Ambrogio Lorenzetti in the 14th century and now lost. It is situated on the first floor, whose rooms have now been turned into a *Civic Museum*. Above the arches giving access to the *Chapel* and *Vestibule* are a series of monochrome frescoes, while the pillars are painted with figures of Sienese *Saints*. On one of the end walls is the large fresco of the Madonna and Child under a canopy borne by Saints known as the "*Maestà*"; it is the first certainly authenticated work of Simone Martini, one of the great protagonists of 14th century painting. On the opposite wall is Simone Martini's other fresco: an equestrian portrait of *Guidoriccio da Fogliano*, celebrating his, victory over the castles of Montemassi and Sassoforte di Maremma, which had rebelled against Siena in 1328. Completed in 1329, the painting formed part of a series of representations of the Castles subjected by the Sienese Republic, now lost. It is dominated at the centre by the figure of the soldier of fortune riding, on his splendidly caparisoned horse, towards the vanquished castles.

The *Chapel*, with 14th century frescoes, is also noteworthy. We then enter the

Sala della Pace, its walls decorated with Ambrogio Lorenzetti's frescoes depicting *Allegories of Good Government and of Bad Government in the City and in the Country* (1327-39). This is followed by the **Sala di Balìa** (or **Sala dei Priori**), and lastly by the **Civic Museum**.

At the base of the **Torre del Mangia** is the **Cappella di Piazza** raised in fulfilment of a vow after the cessation of the plague epidemic in 1348; completed by Giovanni di Cecco, its pillars are adorned with statues of saints.

Beginning a brief tour of the Piazza from the side of the aforementioned Chapel, we come to the **Palazzo Piccolomini**, now the seat of the **Archivio di Stato**; then the **Palazzo Chigi-Zondadari** and **Palazzo Sansedoni**, a massive gothic brick building dating to the first half of the 13th century; it is followed by the rear façade of the **Loggia della Mercanzia**; the **Case de Metz**, and the battlemented **Palazzo d'Elci**. From here, on the left, rises the stairway of the Costarella dei Barbieri, leading into the Via di Città, where at n° 89 we find the **Palazzo Chigi-Saracini**; dating to the 12th century, it is now the seat of the **Chigian Musical Academy**.

Above: *The Town Hall: Guidoriccio da Fogliano by Simone Martini.*
Left: *The Town Hall: Room of the Mappamondo, Christ in Majesty by Simone Martini.*

We turn back a few steps: in the Via del Capitano is the Palace of the Captain of the People, a fine gothic building of the late 13th century, now the seat of the University Faculty of Economic and Banking Sciences. At the end of the street the Piazza del Duomo opens up. It is delimited by the **Hospital of Santa Maria della Scala**, the **Archbishop's Palace**, the **Palazzo della Prefettura** and the **Cathedral** complex. Opposite the Palazzo Pubblico, in the central area of the Campo, is the Renaissance fountain known as the **Fonte Gaia**. It was sculpted by Jacopo della Quercia between 1409 and 1419. Fed by an aqueduct some 25 km. long, the fountain's name derives from the joyful festivities held when the water reached the Piazza del Campo in the 15th century.

PALAZZO SANSEDONI

An imposing brick building of 1216, rebuilt and enlarged by Agostino di Giovanni in 1339, and recently restored. The beautiful façade, whose elegant curve harmonises with the shape of the piazza, is pierced by three orders of three-light mullioned windows, and is surmounted on the left by an unusual rhomboidal tower, which at one time vied in height and elegance with the Torre del Mangia itself.

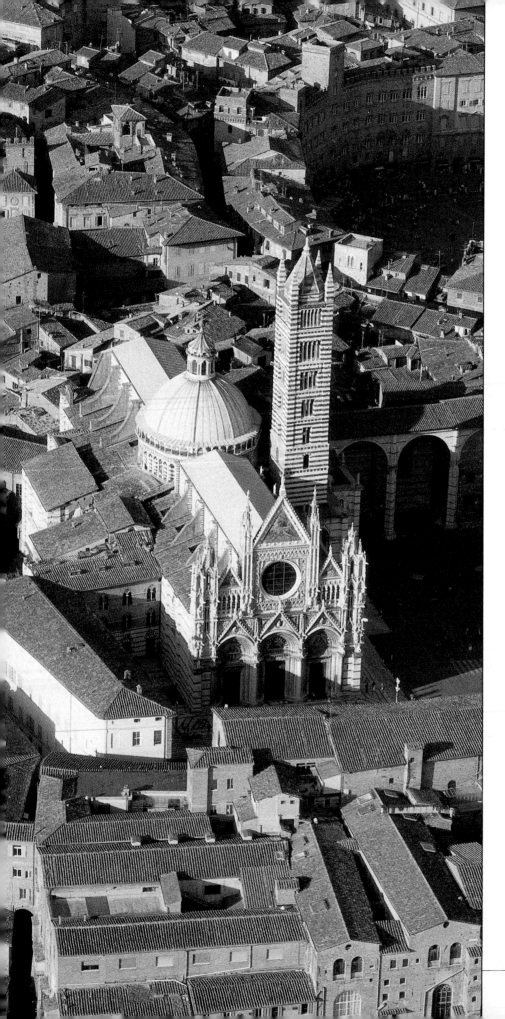

THE CATHEDRAL

Begun in 1229, it was only completed towards the end of the 14th century. By 1264 the central body of the church and the dome had been completed. Giovanni Pisano worked on the façade from 1284 to 1299, but did not get beyond the ground floor. Subsequently further enlargements were planned, but they proved too ambitious and above all too costly, and were speedily abandoned. Attention was then turned to completing the remaining parts of the old Cathedral: in 1382 the apse was completed, and in 1376 Giovanni di Cecco was entrusted with the task of completing the façade. Yet in spite of this chequered history, and the stylistic variations it involved, the Cathedral remains harmonious in appearance and its beauty is intact.

The interior of the Cathedral, lined with alternate courses of black and white marble, is impressive. Pillars supporting round arches divide the nave from the aisles. When we look down at the floor we are faced by another marvel: the **Pavement** is covered with marble **Inlay** and **Graffiti** scenes that reproduce designs of biblical episodes by Pinturicchio, Beccafumi and Matteo di Giovanni (*Massacre of the Innocents*) Among the many masterpieces contained by the Cathedral is Nicola Pisano's beautiful *Pulpit*, which revives and develops the theme of the Pulpit in the Baptistery of Pisa. From inside the Cathedral we can also enter the **Piccolomini Library** (on the left), built for Cardinal Francesco Piccolomini in 1495, and adorned with a complete cycle of frescoes by Pinturicchio. The **Chapel of the Madonna del Voto** in the right transept is adorned with Angels by Lorenzo Bernini. The **Chapel of John the Baptist** in the opposite transept contains the bronze statue of *St. John* by Donatello a late work *the High Altar* was designed by Baldassarre Peruzzi (1552), and is adorned with a *Bronze Ciborium* by Vecchietta and 8 *Angels* by Beccafumi.

Views of the interior of the Duomo and the Pulpitum by Nicola Pisano.

CATHEDRAL MUSEUM

The building which, according to the ambitious original project, was supposed to form the right aisle of the New Cathedral was later transformed into a museum by blocking up the large arches. Founded in 1870 and successively enriched with notable works of art, the Cathedral Museum (Museo dell'Opera Metropolitana) houses a series of precious works of painting and sculpture removed from the Cathedral. On the ground floor are gathered original fragments of architecture and sculpture from the façade and the interior of the Cathedral, most of them attributed to Giovanni Pisano and his school. A *High Relief* by Jacopo della Quercia is placed at the centre of the large room. On the upper floors is an important picture gallery. In the **Room of Duccio**, on the first floor, the famous "*Maestà*", masterpiece of the great Sienese painter, is displayed, together with Pietro Lorenzetti's *Birth of the Virgin* (1342). On the 2nd floor is the early 13th century "*Madonna of the Large Eyes*". It was before it that the people of Siena knelt to pray before the Battle of Montaperti in 1260. From this room a little stairway leads up to the top of the façade of the New Cathedral, from which one of the finest panoramic views of the city can be enjoyed.

On this page: *Museo dell'Opera, ground floor.*
Right-hand page: *Duccio's "Maestà".*

THE BAPTISTERY OR PARISH CHURCH OF SAN GIOVANNI

Its elegant façade attributed to Giacomo di Mino del Pellicciaio is built in white and polychrome marbles, with three large portals. The rectangular interior, with a nave and two aisles, was completed by Tino di Camaino in c. 1325. At its centre is placed the *Baptismal Font*, a wonderful creation of Jacopo della Quercia (1417). Its cornice is decorated with bronze putti by Donatello and one by Giovanni di Turino (1424). Of considerable artistic importance are the six statues and six gilt bronze panels that adorn the sides of the Font; they were sculpted by Jacopo della Quercia, Giovanni di Turino, Turino di Sano, Lorenzo Ghiberti and Donatello.

Interior of the Baptistery with the Font.

PINACOTECA NAZIONALE

At the end of the Via di Città, in the Via San Pietro, is the **Palazzo Buonsignori** a wonderful brick building in the gothic style dating to the 14th-15th century, with two storeys of elegant mullioned windows and a battlemented roofline. Here Siena's main picture gallery, the Pinacoteca Nazionale, is situated. On display in this museum, in chronological order and arranged by artist, is the most substantial group of panel paintings of the

Sienese school from the 13th to the 16th century. The collection was begun by the Abbé Giuseppe Ciaccheri in the 18th century. In 1816 the Abbé De Angelis decided to arrange Ciaccheri's collection in chronological order and to display the works in the premises of the Institute of Fine Arts in the Via della Sapienza. The paintings were later reordered by the superintendent Alessandro Saracini, and then by the art historian Carlo Pini. In March 1915 the nobleman Niccolò Buonsignori bequeathed his own palace in the Via San Pietro to the Provincial Administration of Siena, provided that the latter pledged to convert the building into a museum or picture gallery. Subsequently, after numerous new accessions of important works, the **Museum** was definitively transferred to the State in 1930. At the present time the transfer of the collection to a larger and more suitable venue, i.e. that of the Hospital of Santa Maria della Scala in the Piazza del Duomo, is at the planning stage.

The works of major importance displayed in the gallery are: the *Madonna of the Franciscans*, masterpiece of Duccio di Buoninsegna; a *Madonna and Child* by Simone Martini; two small landscapes by Ambrogio Lorenzetti, *the City by the Sea and Castle on the Banks of a Lake*; a beautiful *Madonna and Child with Saints* and an *Annunciation* by the same artist; a *Christ at the Column* by Sodoma; and a *Holy Family* by Pinturicchio. Works by Sassetta, Sano di Pietro, Ugolino di Nerio, Beccafumi, Francesco Vanni, Albrecht Dürer and others are also on display. After visiting the Palazzo Pubblico and the Cathe-

Left-hand page:
*The Holy
Family with the
infant St.John
Baptist by
Perugino.*

On this page,
right: *Adoration
of the
Shepherds by
Taddeo di
Bartolo.*
Below: *Last
Supper by
Stefano di
Giovanni,
know as
Sassetta.*

dral, we have seen the two main monuments. But Siena is full of many other important monuments, palaces, and churches, which we find scattered throughout the narrow, picturesque streets and little piazzas of the city.

In the Piazza Salimbeni is the 14th century **Palazzo Salimbeni**, a crenellated Gothic building with narrow three-light mullioned windows. It is the seat of the **Monte dei Paschi di Siena**, Italy's oldest banking house. It is faced to the right by the **Palazzo Spannocchi** and to the left by the **Palazzo Tantucci**, both of the 15th century. Nearby is the **Palazzo Tolomei** (12th century); built in grey stone in the gothic style, it is one of the oldest Sienese palaces. It is faced in the same piazza by the **Church of San Cristoforo** of Romanesque origin: it was here that the Council of the Republic met before the Palazzo Pubblico was built. Also in the centre of the city, in the Via S. Virgilio, is the **University**.

The building in which it is housed dates to the 13th century.

In the Piazza San Francesco is the handsome large **Basilica** dedicated to St. Francis; its interior has an Egyptiancross plan, without aisles. Works of sculpture and painting by Pietro and Ambrogio Lorenzetti and Andrea Vanni are preserved in it.

Designed by Agostino di Agnolo in 1320, the church was not completed till the 15th century. Another important church is that of **Santa Maria dei Servi** of the 13th century, but remodelled and transformed in the 15th and 16th. It contains numerous works by Sienese artists, including Coppo di Marcovaldo's *Madonna and Child* and two versions of the *Massacre of the Innocents* by Matteo di Giovanni and Pietro Lorenzetti. Nearby is the **Church of San Girolamo** containing a work by Sano di Pietro (1465). Interesting too is the **Oratory of St. Bernardine**, built in honour of the Saint in the 15th century and containing works by Jacopo della Quercia, Sano di Pietro and Giovanni d'Agostino. The ceiling of the upper room was decorated by Ventura Terapilli; paintings by Sodoma, Beccafumi and Gerolamo Pacchia are also present. In the Via del Giglio is the **Church of San Pietro in Ovile**, its existing construction dating to 1753. Inside is an *Annunciation*, a fine imitation of the original by Simone Martini. In the Piazza Provenzano Salvani stands the **church of Santa Maria in Provenzano**, designed by Flaminia del Turco in 1594 and built in a late Renaissance stule. The venerated 13th century icon known as the *Madonna of Provenzano* is protected in a sumptuous tabernacle on the high altar. Siena is spread out on three hills, delimited by the Arbia and Elsa valleys. These hills, or ridges, join together in the area

Above:
Fonte Branda.
Right:
Piazza Salimbeni.
Right-hand page:
The Basilica of San Domenico: Chapel of Saint Catherine.

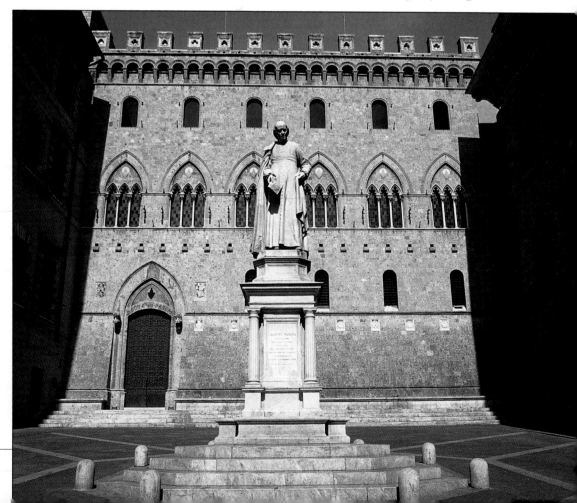

now occupied by the Campo, thus assuming the shape of an upside down Y. Reflecting this tripartite topography, the city itself is divided into three **Terzi** or **Terzieri**: the Terzo di **Città**, that of **San Martino** and that of **Camollia** which comprise in turn the 17 **Contrade** or urban districts, each with its own banner and its own church.

The medieval centre is well defended by seven kilometres of thick walls pierced by a number of gates and by the **Fort of St. Barbara** or **Medici Fortress**, constructed by Cosimo I in 1560. The fort consists of a huge rectangle with massive bulwarks at the corners; the ramparts, transformed into a public park in 1937, provide fine panoramic views over the city and the surrounding hills. On the eastern side of the city the walls are pierced by the gate in the Via Fontebranda, at the foot of the hill on which the Basilica of San Domenico stands. Almost facing it is the monumental **Fonte Branda**.

It is the most famous of the many Sienese public fountains.

It already existed in 1081; it was enlarged by Bellarmino later; and given its present appearance by Giovanni di Stefano in 1246. It has something of the appearance of a miniature fortress, brick-built with three large gothic arches surmounted by elegant tympana, adorned with crenellations; in front are four lion gargoyles, with the coat of arms of Siena in the middle.

To the right of the fountain begins the narrow alley called the Vicolo del Tiratoio, on which is situated the **House of Saint Catherine**.

The entrance to the complex that has developed round it, the **Sanctuary of Saint Catherine**, is at n° 15. It consists of the **Upper Oratory** (kitchen of St. Catherine), the **Lower Oratory** (workshop of her father), the **Oratory of the Chamber** (Saint's Room), and the **Church of the Crucifix** (over the garden of the house). In the Upper Oratory we may see the remains of the ancient hearth, the fine floor and the wooden coffered ceiling. Along the walls are placed 17 pictures illustrating various episodes from the life of the Saint. Adjacent to the Oratory is the **Cell** in which the Saint lived and in which objects belonging to her, including the stone she used as a pillow, are preserved. She was canonized by Pius II in 1461, and proclaimed Co-Patron of Italy by Pius XII on 30 April 1939.

BASILICA OF SAN DOMENICO

Impressive in appearance, especially on the side that rises sheer from the gorge of Fonte Branda, this large basilica too is in the gothic style. It was begun in 1225 and completed in 1465. A succession of alterations were made later, but the church has now been restored to its original austere appearance by a series of restorations, the last of which was the reopening of the large three-light mullioned windows.

Inside it consists of a single nave. In the **Chapel of the Vaults** is a portrait of Saint Catherine by Andrea Vanni (1322-1414); it is believed to be the only faithful portrait of the Saint. In the **Chapel of the Saint** (1488) her mummified head is preserved, and the walls are frescoed by Sodoma and Francesco Vanni, depicting *the Ecstasy of St. Catherine*, *the* Swoon *of St. Catherine* and *the Healing of the Possessed*.

Other paintings by Sano di Pietro, Matteo di Giovanni, Benvenuto di Giovanni and Pietro Lorenzetti decorate the transepts and the other two chapels. A road on the left leads down to the **Crypt**, dating to the 14th century. To the right of the façade of San Domenico is the 15th century **Cloister** with recently rediscovered frescoes by Lippo Memmi.

By taking the Viale dei Mille from the piazza in front of San Domenico, we can reach the massive **Bastions of the Medici Fortress**.

THE PALIO

Even though the evidence on the origins and early history of the Palio of Siena is scant and indirect, it is certain that this festivity, the most popular and famous of the city, already existed before 1310, the year in which a document of the General Council of Siena consecrated the official establishment of the Palio "to be run on 16th August in honour of the Blessed Virgin". And if originally the mid-August Palio was only the crowning moment of a popular festivity, it came to assume, after the battle of Montaperti in 1260, and the victory of the Sienese people over the Florentines, an ever growing importance and even a political significance. On the other hand, it was only in 1656 that the institution of a second Palio, the "Palio of the Contrade" "run on the 2nd July in honour of the Madonna di Provenzano", was officially recognised. The Sienese Contrade (urban districts), originally some 80 in all, but gradually reduced in number to the current 17, do not only have a representative role today, nor is their life exhausted exclusively in the preparation and realization of the Palio. The Palio is in fact something more than a mere folkloric spectacle or an historical reevocation in period costumes. Today as in the past the Palio is the festivity of Siena and its seventeen Contrade which compete among each other for the coveted painted silk banner (i.e. the Palio itself). It is a kind of rite in which Siena reveals her true face and relives, with passion and nostalgia, a wonderful dream of past greatness. The "***Mossa***", or the start of the horserace in the Campo. It is the most emotional and complex moment of the Palio. There are the ten jockeys, mounted on their beautiful Barbary horses, they too excited and anxiously waiting to go. On coming through the "Entrone", the portal that admits into the Cortile del Podestà, they are

handed the leather whip with which to incite their steed and strike at their adversary jockeys and horses. They approach the point of departure: the "Mossa!", and they are off; barely has the startingwire touched the

ground before the ten horses are launched on their pellmell course round the Campo. Horse and rider become as one, tensed together in this dramatic and hurtling struggle. The enthusiasm of the supporters of the various Contrade explodes uncontainably, and involves everyone. One round, two rounds have passed, only a few Contrade are still left in the running. The last curve approaches, that of San Martino, the most dangerous of all, then the straight up to the finishing line! The race has been hard fought right up to the black and white flag that marks its end. Shouts of jubilation greet the victors, groans the losers.

THE CHIANTI COUNTRY

Enclosed between the provinces of Siena and Florence, the Chianti Country is an harmonious territory, feudal in aspect, covering some 70,000 hectares. A succession of isolated farmhouses, fortified settlements, castles, towers, abbeys and parish churches are scattered over its hills. The etymology of **Chianti** is disputed: it may derive from "*Clango*" (sounds made by a horn), or from the Etruscan "*Clante-i*". It is, however, certain, given the numerous fossil vines found at San Vivaldo and the evidence for Etruscan wine consumption, that the area was inhabited by the Etruscans who were perhaps the first to plant vines.

Undoubtedly wine was produced in the Etruscan and Roman periods.

But the first documents on wine production date to 913 (Chiesa di Santa Cristina at Lucignano) and 1037 (Badia Coltibuono). In the mid-18th century the introduction of a new

receptacle, the "fiasco" - the characteristic straw-covered flask of Chianti - increased its fame and was to become its symbol. The most important centres of Chianti are **Greve in Chianti**, **Gaiole in Chianti**, **Castellina**, one of the highest of the Chianti centres with its ancient Fortress, and **Radda in Chianti** with its ancient church.   Apart from the main centres, the territory is dotted with picturesque small villages and, on its hilltops, with numerous castles such as those of **Brolio**, **Cacchiano**, **Tornano**, **Meleto**, **Volpaia**, **Spaltenna** and the **Villa Vistarenni** in which, as in the numerous recently restored farmhouses, the wine of Chianti is produced from the grapes gathered from their own vineyards.

As early as 1716 the Grand Duke of Tuscany, Pietro Leopoldo, proclaimed Chianti a **"wine of protected denomination and origin"**. Today it is famous throughout the world.

SAN GIMIGNANO

The "city of the beautiful towers" stands in a picturesque position on a hill dominating the Val d'Elsa, once inhabited by the Etruscans. San Gimignano experienced its most fortunate period in the late Middle Ages, with the flowering of urban civilization; the double circuit of walls, the gates, the fountains, the big town houses and the massive stone towers date to the communal period.

Thereafter, as a result of the fierce civil strife that developed inside the town, and the growing power of the other Tuscan cities, especially Siena and Florence, San Gimignano embarked on a long period of decadence. Yet for this very reason its beautiful 13th and 14th century fabric has been preserved virtually intact: its piazzas guarded by ancient buildings, its narrow and shaded little alleys still paved in herringbone patterns, its forest of towers which constitutes the most characteristic note of the town. Of the 72 towers that once soared into the skies of San Gimignano, only 15 intact ones still survive today.

Yet they represent one of the most vivid and striking records of Tuscan life in the Middle Ages. The town centre is represented by the picturesque and luminous *Piazza della Cisterna*, surrounded by ancient palaces and towers such as the *Casa Razzi*, *Casa Silvestrini* and *Palazzo Tortoli* on the south side; to the north is the *Palazzo Cortesi* with the tall *Torre del Diavolo*.

Piazza della Cisterna.

On its east side the piazza is flanked by the **Case Semplici**, warehouses and another tower, the 13th century **Torre degli Ardinghelli**. Placed over a massive stepped podium is the **Cisterna** or public fountain that the piazza is named after; it was erected in 1273.

At the foot of the Via del Castello is the **Church of SanLorenzo in Ponte** (13th century), with interesting frescoes by a 15th century Florentine painter.

THE CATHEDRAL

On the west side of the Piazza del **Duomo**, which together with the adjoining Piazza della Cisterna constitutes the monumental centre of San Gimignano, stands the Cathedral or Collegiata. This church is a distinguished monument of Romanesque architecture in Tuscany. Its aisles are decorated with cycles of frescoes: the left aisle with *Episodes from the Old Testament* by Bartolo di Fredi (c. 1367); and the right aisle with *Episodes from the New Testament* by the great Barna da Siena. The entrance wall, against which are placed the two famous painted *Wooden Statues of Mary and the Angel Gabriel* by Jacopo della Quercia, is frescoed by Taddeo di Bartolo with scenes of the *Last Judgement, Heaven* and *Hell*. Below the Last Judgement is Benozzo Gozzoli's painting of the *Martyrdom of St. Sebastian* (1465).

Facing the Cathedral, in the same piazza, is the **Palazzo del Podestà** (12391337) with its **Tower** (Torre Rognosa). On the left side of the Cathedral is the **Palazzo del Popolo** of 1288, now the Town Hall. On its right rises the **Torre Grossa** (54 m.). The building also houses the **Civic Museums** and **Picture Gallery**.

CIVIC MUSEUM

The Museum is entered from the courtyard of the Palazzo del Popolo. It contains the collections of art owned by the municipality and largely coming from other buildings in San Gimignano.

First we enter the **Sala di Dante,** so called because it was here that Dante addressed the Podestà and General Council in 1300, urging the need for a Guelf league in Tuscany.

But what expecially makes this room famous, and immediately draws the visitor's attention, is the great *"Maestà"* painted by Lippo Memmi on the right wall.

Other paintings adorn the walls of this room: on the end wall is a fresco which seems to represent the *Oath of Fidelity* to Charles of Anjou, while the other walls are frescoed with sadly much deteriorated *Scenes of Hunting, Submissions of Castles, Jousts* and *Tournaments of Knights,* dating to the end of the 13th century and attributed to a Sienese painter called Azzo.

Above: *Our Lady enthroned with the Child and two saints by Benozzo Gozzoli.*
Below: *Christ in Majesty by Lippo Memmi.*

The upper floors of the Palazzo del Popolo house the **Pinacoteca Civica** (Civic Picture Gallery), a highly important collection of paintings of the Sienese and Florentine schools from the 13th to the 15th century. They include works by Filippino Lippi (the two tondos of the *Annunciation*), Pinturicchio, Coppo di Marcovaldo, Benozzo Gozzoli and Niccolò Gerini (*8 Episodes from the Life of Saint Fina*). From the Gallery it is possible to climb to the top of San Gimignano's highest Tower (the Torre Grossa) which commands magnificent views of the city below and its surrounding hills.

CHURCH OF SANT'AGOSTINO

From the Porta San Matteo, by the characteristic Via Cellolese, we may reach the Piazza Sant'Agostino, dominated by the church dedicated to the Saint. Built together with its adjoining convent (now suppressed) in a Romanesque-Gothic style between 1280 and 1298, the church with its simple façade still presents traces of its original architecture. But the real treasure of the church consists of the various frescoes that decorate its interior, notably the large cycle of the *Life of St. Augustine* by Benozzo Gozzoli that entirely covers the walls of the choir. Other paintings include the **Chapel of San Bartolo** painted by the Sienese painter Sebastiano Mainardi (1500); works by Bartolo di Fredi, Tamagni and Lippo Memmi. Noteworthy, too, is Pietro del Pollaiolo's painting of the *Coronation of the Virgin with Saints* over the High Altar.

Also worth visiting in the historic centre of the town are the churches of **San Bartolo** and **San Jacopo**, while just out side the town, in a particularly scenic spot, is the small Romanesque **Church of Cellole.**

CHIANCIANO TERME

One of Italy's most famous spas, ***Chianciano Terme*** occupies a truly magnificent position on the hills that descend to the Val di Chiana. The history of these springs is very ancient: the Etruscans and Romans already benefited from the health-giving waters that flow so copiously in the area. Yet it is only in recent times that the therapeutic properties of these sulphuric calcipherous waters have been suitably exploited. Today Chianciano Terme is an elegant modern town, consisting largely of hotels and boarding-houses, and spacious tree-lined avenues flanked by shops, cafés and flower-beds. The spa facilities themselves are to be found in a number of scenic parks. They are organized according to the most advanced criteria. The largest of them is that of the ***Fonte dell'Acqua Santa*** (Holy Water Springs) situated in the beautiful Parco delle Fonti and Parco Fucoli.

Also comprised by the hydro-mineral area of Chianciano Terme is the ***Source of Saint Helena***, named after the ancient Chapel of Saint Helena close to which the water had its spring. The historic centre of Chianciano stands on a panoramic hilltop not far from the modern spa.

Probably Etruscan in origin, it is surrounded in part by medieval walls.

The town layout is typically medieval, with numerous picturesque alleyways radiating out from the town centre towards the outer "***Vie delle Mura***".

On entering the town through the 16th century Porta Rivellini, we take the Via Casini which brings us to the ***Torre dell'Orologio*** (Clock Tower) with the Medici coat of arms. A few steps to the left we enter the Piazza del Comune (or Piazza Matteotti), adorned by a handsome 18th century fountain. Also of interest is a visit to the Collegiata church, the Museum of Sacred Art in the Palazzo dell'Arcipretura and the nearby 13th century Palazzo del Podestà, adorned with coats of arms of the 15th and 16th centuries. A highly modern sports centre, equipped with Olympicsize swimming pools and trampoline, was recently inaugurated in an extensive area of parkland.

MONTEPULCIANO

A town of very ancient origins, it was inhabited by the Etruscans; indeed legend recounts that it was founded by King Porsenna. Recorded with the name *Mons Politianus* in 715, Montepulciano was involved in the Middle Ages in the protracted struggles that divided Arezzo, Florence and Siena. Claimed by each, it was not until the 15th and 16th century that it could enjoy a long period of peace. Many important palaces and churches can ben encountered on the street that ascends to the town centre in the Piazza Grande: the **Palazzo Avignonesi** designed by Vignola; the **church of Sant'Agostino** by Michelozzo, situated opposite the tower known as the **Torre del Pulcinella**; the handsome **Palazzo Cervini**, desigend by Sangallo. In the upper part of the town is the **House of Politian** and the 14th century **church of SantaMaria dei Servi**. From here we can ascend to the **Fortress**, and then by way of the Via Fiorenzuola enter the Piazza Grande. The **Piazza Grande** represents the monumental centre of the town. It is flanked by the **Cathedral**, erected by Ippolito Scalza between 1592 and 1630; the 14th century **Palazzo Comunale**; the Palazzo Contucci designed by Antonio da Sangallo the Elder; the **Palazzo Tarugi** designed by Vignola. In the centre of the piazza is the characteristic **Fountains of Griffins and Lions**. The tower at its centre commands fine views of the town and its environs. Over the high altar in the Cathedral is the great triptych of the *Assumption* (1401) by Taddeo di Bartolo, the most important Sienese painter of the late 14th century. In the central panel we see the Assumption and Coronation of Mary. To the left: the Saints most venerated in Montepulciano; the Archangel Gabriel, the female Saints and the Annunciate Mary. On the four pilasters are the 12 Apostles and in the predella panel at the bottom Scenes from the Life of Jesus and episodes from the Bible. Isolated at the foot of the hill on which Montepulciano stands is the **Basilica of the Madonna of San Biagio**, a masterpiece of Renaissance architecture by Sangallo the Elder.

Above: *Detail of the Torre di Pulcinella.*
Right:
Town Hall and PalazzoTarugi.

131

Left: *Piazza Grande - Town Hall, the Well of the Grifons and Lions.*
Below: *The Duomo.*
Right: *The Basilica of the Madonna of San Biagio.*

Montepulciano, interior of the Basilica of the Madonna of San Biagio.

PIENZA

Close to Montepulciano is the small town of Pienza, one of the most interesting in Italy from an urbanistic point of view. It was designed and built by Bernardo Rossellino, a rare example of Renaissance town-planning. In the central piazza, or Piazza Pio II, is the **Cathedral**, which contains paintings by **Matteo di Giovanni**, **Vecchietta** and **Sano di Pietro**. It was again designed by Rossellino. Flanking the Cathedral on the right is the **Palazzo Piccolomini**, another splendid building by Rossellino (1459-62), with a wonderful square courtyard and a scenic hanging garden. On the left side is the Canons' House, a Renaissance building that now houses the **Cathedral Museum**. Facing the Cathedral is the **Palazzo Comunale** with a brick battlemented tower.

Not far from Pienza, beyond Torrenieri, is **San Quirico d'Orcia** with its ancient **Parish Church** (Collegiata or Pieve di Orsenna), mentioned in the 8th century and reconstructed in the 12th. From Torrenieri, a small agricultural town, the road ascends gently to the top of the hill on which **Montalcino** is laid out. Its late-medieval architecture ia of clearly Sienese inspiration.

The Cathedral of Pienza.

Overlooking the central Piazza del Popolo is the **Loggia** with its gothic arches (14th-15th century) and the **Palazzo Comunale**, the former **Palazzo dei Priori** (13th-14th century). Its high tower in stone and brick is adorned with numerous coats of arms. The town is dominated by the Fortress (Rocca) at the top of the hill: an important model of military architecture and the last bulwark of Sienese liberty. Not far from the town is the 11th century **Abbey of Sant'Antimo**, with a wonderful Romaneseque interior.

In the vicinity of Siena, on the provincial highway that leads to Follonica, is another fine abbey: the **Abbey of San Galgano**, whose ruins represent the most illustrious Gothic Cistercian monument in Italy after those of Fossanova and Casamari in Lazio. On its right is the **Monastery** with the **Chapter House**, **Monks' Room**, the 16 cells of the monks and the **Monks' Choir.**

The Palazzo Piccolomini.

AREZZO

This ancient and noble city lies on the gentle slope of a hill, with the green mountains of the Casentino at its back, and overlooking the fertile plain between the valleys of the Tiber, Arno and Chiana.

One of the 12 confederate cities of Etruria when Rome had not yet been born, the ancient Arretium's fortune did not decline in the Roman period; Maecenas, the friend and protector of Horace and Virgil, was Aretine. Among the first Italian cities to set itself up as a republic, medieval Arezzo enjoyed centuries of prosperity through trade and banking activity.

And even when, in the late 14th century, it finally succumbed to Florentine rule, it continued to maintain a leading position, thanks to men who played such an important role in Italian culture: Petrarch was a native of Arezzo, as was Vasari, while Michelangelo was born at Caprese nearby.

One of the most picturesque spots in the town is the Piazza Grande, where the is held spectacular jousting contest known as the **Giostra del Saracino**. It is surrounded by medieval houses and towers, by the imposing **Palazzo delle Logge**, and by the elegant gothic façade of the Palazzo della Fraternità dei Laici. At the centre of the piazza stands the 15th century **Public Fountain**. Also looking onto the piazza is the semicircular apse of the **church of Santa Maria**, one of the masterpieces of the Romanesque in Tuscany; in the plate to the right, the severe facade of the church, erected in the 13th century and flanked by a sturdy bell-tower.

The interior consists of a nave and aisles, and contains some notable works of art, including the celebrated *Polyptych of Pietro Lorenzetti* (1320) on the high altar; a fresco with *Saints Francis and Domenic* by an artist of the school of Giotto (early 14th century); and a fine *Crucifix* painted by Margarito d'Arezzo.

The **Cathedral**, an imposing gothic building dating to the 13th century, is situated close to the Piazza Grande. Standing over a 16th century stairway, its ancient façade, never completed, was replaced by the existing neogothic facade designed by Dante Viviani and erected in 1901-14. The spacious interior contains important *Stained Glass*, and a number of works of art, including Piero della Francesca's famous fresco of the *Magdalen*.

Between the Duomo and the Piazza Grande is the **House of Petrarch**. Built in the 16th century over a medieval building and recently restored, it is

now the seat of the **Petrarch Academy of Letters and Scienze**. Close to the railway station, in the Via Margaritone, is the entrance to the **Roman Amphitheatre**, which dates to the late 1st century B. C. Elliptical in shape, it could accommodate over 8000 spectators. Other noteworthy monuments are to be seen in the city: the 13th century **Basilica of San Francesco** with frescoes by Piero della Francesca; and the Church **of San Domenico**, which contains a superb youthful work by **Cimabue** (1260-65) over its high altar. On the Via XX Settembre, at n° 55, is the House of Giorgio Vasari, with its **Vasarian Museum and Archive**.

Left-hand page:
*Detail of the
Façade of the
Parish Church.*
On this page:
*Interior of the
Parish Church.*

Left: *The Cathedral.*
Below: *Palazzo Comunale.*

Also in the centre of the town is the Renaissance **Palazzo Bruni-Ciocchi** on the Via San Lorentino; it contains the **Medieval and Moderm Gallery and Museum**.

Mentioned as early as 1593, but certainly of yet earlier origin, the **Giostra del Saracino** is a horseback contest held in the Piazza Grande. The horsemen who represent the Four Quarters of the town must strike the target represented by the model of an armed Saracen with their lance as they gallop past; the winner is the one who comes closest to the bull's eye of striking the centre of the Saracen's shield.

The prize is the "Golden Lance". A historic procession in rich period costumes precedes the contest.

In the background of the photo is the **Palazzo Comunale**, built in 1333 as the **Palazzo dei Priori**, with a medieval tower; the clock dates to 1468.

Inside there is an arcaded courtyard, and two rooms, the **Sala dei Matrimoni** and **Sala del Consiglio**, frescoed by Giorgio Vasari, Parri di Spinello and Sebastiano del Piombo.

CORTONA

A small but fascinating town of Etruscan origin, Cortona is huddled on the slope of a hill dominated by the 16th century **Medici Fortress**. The structure of the medieval city, together with fine examples of Renaissance architecture, have been magnificently preserved. The piazza that forms its centre is flanked by the 13th century **Palazzo Comunale**, which contains a beautiful **Council Hall**. At n° 9 of the same piazza is the **Palazzo Pretorio**, built in the 13th century as the residence of the Casali family, but with a façade added by Filippo Berrettini (cousin of Pietro da Cortona) in 1613. It now houses **the Academy and Museum of the Etruscan Academy**. Its exhibits include the famous Etruscan *bronze Candelabrum*, dating to the 5th century B.C. and 58 kg. in weight; the *Muse Polymnia*, an original Graeco-Roman painting on slate dating to the 1st-2nd century; a funerary *Boat Model* of the 12th Egyptian Dynasty; and a large *Crucifix* of the 13th century Pisan school. Other objects are housed in the museum such as paintings, two mummies with sarcophagi of the 4th century B.C., coins, medals and so on.

Just a few steps away is the **Cathedral**, erected over the remains of the ancient Romanesque church of Santa Maria, and based on designs by Giuliano da Sangallo and his followers. On the high altar is a fine **Tabernacle** by Francesco Mazzuoli (1664). The apse is decorated with paintings by Cigoli and the school of Signorelli. Facing it is the former **Church of the Gesù**, which now houses the **Diocesan Museum** comprising a distinguished collection of paintings by Tuscan old masters.

Of particular interest is Fra Angelico's splendid *Annunciation*, and a *Crucifix* by Pietro Lorenzetti. There are also works by Sassetta, Signorelli and others among the numerous other paintings.

In the gothic **Church of San-Francesco** (13th century) is a fine paintings by Cigoli depicting *St. Anthony of Padua and the Miracle of the Mule*. Noteworthy, too, are Raffaele Vanni's *Nativity*, and Pietro da Cortona's uncompleted *Annunciation*.

Above: *The Duomo*.
Right: *The Town Hall*.

SAN SEPOLCRO

Situated to the east of Arezzo, it can be reached in less than an hour. A commercial and industrial centre, its name derives from the tradition that two pilgrims, Arcanus and Egidius, founded an oratory here to house some relics of the Holy Sepulchre. Sansepolcro was the birthplace of Piero della Francesca (1420-1492) and the painters Matteo di Giovanni, Raffaellino del Colle and Cristoforo Gherardi known as Il Doceno (1508-1556); of Luca Pacioli, a distinguished mathematician; and the numerous family of the Alberti composed of architects, painters and sculptors. The centre of the town is marked by the Piazza Torre di Berta. From there, by the Via dei Servi, we reach the **church of Santa Maria dei Servi** with gothic traces of the 13th century. By the Via Mattotti we reach the **Cathedral**. Built in a mixed Romanesque-Gothic style as the abbey of the Camaldolensians in the 11th century, it was rebuilt in the 14th. The façade is adorned with a fine portal of Lombard type and a large rose window. The interior, with a nave and two aisles, contains a number of paintings and frescoes, and a magnificent statue of the *Madonna and Child*, a Florentine work of the 14th century. The Palazzo Comunale, of 14th century origin, houses the **Picture Gallery** (Pinacoteca); the paintings on display include Piero della Francesca's wonderful fresco of the *Resurrection*, painted in 1463. A selfportrait of the artist has been detected by some in the second figure from the left, facing frontally but with closed eyes.

The City Museum: Polyptych of the Misericordia by Piero della Francesca.

*City Museum:
Nativity Scene
by Andrea della
Robbia.*

CAPRESE

North of Sansepolcro is Caprese Michelangelo, a small hill-town, in which is situated the house where its most famous citizen, **Michelangelo Buonarroti**, was born on 6 March 1475. Chiusi della Verna disputed with Caprese the honour of having given birth to the great artist, resting its claims on the dubious words of Vasari.

But the discovery in 1875 of a copy of the birth certificate written by Michelangelo's father settled the long controversy in favour of Caprese.

Recorded for the first time after the year 1000, Caprese was a fief of the Lords of Galbino, then of the Camaldolensians, then (from 1260) of the Guidi di Romena.

Besieged and conquered by the Tarlati of Arezzo, the town voluntarily submitted itself to Florence in 1384. It is still dominated by the ruins of its 14th century castle.

House of Michelangelo Buonarroti.

FRANCISCAN SANCTUARY OF LA VERNA

On the slopes of Monte Penna, 4 km. from Chiusi della Verna, a popular holiday resort, is the great *Sanctuary* whose rude and massive appearance is imbued with the memories of the time spent here by the **Saint of Assisi**. It was Count Orlando dei Cattani, owner of the mountain, then an uninhabited wilderness, who donated it to St. Francis in 1213. Francis went there with some of his companions two years later and built wattle-and-daub huts for them to clive in.

Francis returned to La Verna in 1216; it was then, while walking over the mountain, that he found a cave where he later came to pray, sometimes resting by sitting on a rock.

In the following years the Saint visited the Hermitage on other occasions and it was there, on 17 September 1224, that he received the stigmata.

The precise spot of the miracle is marked today by a bronze grate in the floor of the **Chapel of the Stigmata**, erected in 1263. On passing through the archway in the rock, on ascending to La Verna, we first come to the little **Church of Santa Maria degli Angeli**, built by St. Francis with the help of Count Orlandi (1216-18). The interior consists of a single nave with two altars: to the right is a *Pietà* and a *Madonna and Child with Saints*; to the left, the Adoration of the Child and Saints Francis and Anthony of Padua.

There is a beautiful altar frontal of glazed terracotta representing the *Assumption of Mary* by Andrea della Robbia. A stone at the centre marks the burial place of Count Orlando Cattani. In the **Major Church** or Basilica is the Chapel of the Conception (or of the Relics).

In the shrine of the *Nativity* is another magnificent terracotta by Andrea della Robbia representing the *Adoration* (1479). Other fine terracottas by the same master adorn the church: the *Virgin in Adoration* , *St. Anthony Abbot* and *St. Francis*, the *Ascension*, and the *Anunciation*.

By a small door we enter the Corridor of the Stigmata, then the Grotto where the Saint prayed and the Cell of St. Francis. From there we can continue by entering the Church of the Stigmata, the heart of the Sanctuary, built by Count Simone da Battifolle in 1263; it too contains numerous works by Andrea della Robbia.

A Pietà by della Robbia School and the Corridor of the Stigmata.

Interior of Santa Maria degli Angeli.

HERMITAGE OF CAMALDOLI

The original nucleus of the Sanctuary comprises the **Monastery** and its adjacent buildings. Then came the **Hermitage**, three kilometres away, in the midst of the dense forest. It dates to 1012 when St. Romuald was donated the territory by Count Maldolo d'Arezzo, and constructed the first nucleus of the Hermitage. On the death of the Saint in 1027, the congregation had already expanded, and in 1080 the Blessed Rodolfo drew up its rules. Today the Congregation, comprising the Camaldolensian hermit monks of the Order of St. Benedict, practice the contemplative life, uniting the cenobitic with the eremitic regime. To the left of the entrance is the **Chapel of St. Anthony**, while on the far side of the piazza is the front of the **Church of the Saviour**, consecrated in 1027, enlarged and remodelled in 1658. Beyond a wroughtiron gate is the suggestive enclosure of the 20 Cellsinhabited by the monks.

The Benedictine Monastery of Vallombrosa, founded by Giovanni Gualberti in 1051, is situated not very far from Camaldoli, bordering on the province of Arezzo and in the midst of a forest of beech, chestnut and pine. The existing building of the Monastery dates to the 15th century. Grand and austere, with its 15th century tower, it has the appearance of a castle. By a wide portal we enter a small courtyard where the church is situated. It dates to 1664. Of great interest in its interior is the **Chapel of St. Paul**, now the **Baptistery**, with paintings and frescoes of the 17th-l8th century.

Church of the Salvatore.

POPPI

If La Verna and Camaldoli are the religious and ascetic symbol of the Casentino, Poppi, with its **Castle** or **Palazzo Pretorio**, is its lay and feudal symbol, visible like La Verna from a great distance. This impregnable building, which truly dominates the whole region, recorded from 1169 on, was the cradle and main residence of the Conti Guidi, who moved there from Battifolle and turned it into the capital of their best known and most enduring feud. The last lord of the Castle was count Francesco who, having allied himself with the Duke of Milan against the Florentines in 1440, was banned from his lands after the battle of Anghiari.

Poppi then passed definitiveiy under Florentine control. Today Poppi is a charming little town, situated on top of an isolated hill, on the right bank of the Arno in the heart of the Casentino. In the piazza Amerighi is the **Church of the Madonna del Morbo** (17th century), with an elegant dome and arcades that surround it on three sides. The view of the church from the Via Cavour is particularly attractive.

Church of the Madonna del Morbo.

The Castle or Palazzo Pretorio.

GROSSETO

The province of Grosseto is situated at the centre of the Maremma, in the southwestern part of Tuscany. It is one of the most varied and scenic provinces of the region from a landscape point of view, its coastline dotted with picturesque beaches, cliffs, seaside resorts and campsites. A former feud of the Aldobrandeschi, then dominated by the Medici, Grosseto is the capital of the Maremma. It is a lively modern town that is undergoing rapid expansion in the plain around the old town contained within the hexagonal circuit of the Medici walls. It might seem, at first sight, a city that has sprang up in the space of a few decades. But there is the 13th century **Church of San Francesco**, with a picturesque cloister. There is the beautiful **Romanesque Cathedral of San Lorenzo**, restored cfrom 1294 to 1302. There are the 16th century **Medici Walls**, transformed into a public park, which have won the town the reputation as a "little Lucca". Of considerable interest are the Museum of Sacred Art, comprising paintings of the Sienese and Florentine schools, and the Archaeological Museum, which provides a review of the development of civilization in the Maremma from prehistoric to Etruscan times. In fact, this region, prior to the birth of Rome, was the heart of Etruscan civilization. Roselle, Populonia, Vetulonia, Saturnia: all of them ancient cities which, with their ruins and subterranean tombs, perpetuate the mystery: of this civilization. The rich artistic heritage, the legacy of a millennial history, confer a distinctive character on the landscape of the Maremma: the remains of Etruscan cities, monuments of the Roman period, medieval cities which seem to have been frozen in time, all converge in the present to form a truly unique and living reality.

Church of San Francesco, Crucifix by Duccio di Buoninsegna.

DIOCESAN MUSEUM OF SACRED ART
Situated above the Sacristy of the Cathedral, it contains some major works of art removed both from the Cathedral and from other churches in Grosseto and its environs.
Pietro Lorenzetti, Ugolino di Neri, Segna di Bonaventura, Sassetta, Beccafumi and pupils of the school of Sodoma, are just a few of the artists represented in the Museum.

MUSEUM OF ARCHAEOLOGY AND ART OF THE MAREMMA
Reorganized in the classicizing building on the Piazza Baccarini, it gathers together the remains of the prehistoric and historic civilizations of the Maremma. It is divided into the following sections: palaeolithic, protohistoric, Rosellan and topographic. On the second floor are the Dark Age section and the Museum of Art.
It also houses a fine collection of medieval pottery and liturgical objects, and many paintings of the Florentine and Sienese schools up to the 17th century.

The Cathedral (13th-14th century).

ROSELLE

Roselle, an Etruscan city, stands on a hill some 150 m. high on the north-western edge of the plain of Grosseto. Formed, like other cities of Etruria, from the union of various villages of the Villanovan period, Roselle rose to power from the 7th

century B.C. on. It fell into a decline following its defeat at the hands of the Roman consul L. Postumius Megellus in 294 B.C. But it remained inhabited, albeit with a reduced population, throughout the Middle Ages. Its **Cemeteries** contain tombs of various type; they have yielded vases, amphorae, archaic stelae carved with figures, and so on. On this page we see a stretch of the **Etruscan Circuit of Walls**, which have a perimeter of c. 3 km., and enclose the upper part of the town (6th century B.C.); a stretch of **Roman Road** close to the **Forum** and **Amphitheatre** and the remains of a **Building of the Roman Period**.

Etruscan walls and Roman buildings.

NATURE RESERVE OF THE MAREMMA

The nature reserve known as the ***Parco dell'Uccellina*** protects the integrity of the Maremma's environment. The characteristic Macchia - scrubland - in which live roe deer, fallow deer and wild boar, and the remains of prehistoric, Etruscan and medieval settlements, are fused in such a way that it is difficult to distinguish the work of nature from that of man.

In the Maremma, by ably exploiting the local resources, man, from the remote times of the Etruscans, has built towns and villages, and erected walls and fortresses for his own defence. He has also exploited the region's mineral resources: the mines used since bronze age times, especially of copper, iron, cinnabar, silver, etc., have been of great importance.

The Romans too cultivated the fertile fields of this land, deriving riches and power from them.

The Maremma is the name given to the area of southern Tuscany and north-western Lazio that extends from the mouth of the river Cecina in the province of Livorno to beyond Tarquinia in Lazio.

The central zone of this region is called the Maremma Grossetana, and is the one that best preserves its specific characteristics. A particularly striking feature of the area are the herds of semiwild horses that live in groups, as on the prairie. The Maremma can also boast of its local cowboys: these are the famous "**Butteri**" who exhibit their prowess in the "Mer-

ca del bestiame", an event that is normally held on the last Sunday of April and one that revives one of the most vivid traditions of the Maremma, perpetuating the use of hot-iron branding to mark the wild cattle that the Butteri drive from the plains and round up into corrals.

MONTE ARGENTARIO

This is the promontory with a richly wooded interior and a brilliantly rocky coast that stretches into the Tyrrhenian opposite the Islands of Giglio and Giannutri. Joined to the mainland only in historical times, it still preserves its essential character as an island. Along its coast, which is very jagged, a series of enchanting bays, beaches, cliffs, precipices and caves open up. Its remote and more recent seafaring tradition is borne witness to by the tutelary deities of the two towns that stand on opposite sides of the promontory: Porto Ercole, the God of seafaring Etruscans, and Porto Santo Stefano, the Saint who protects sailors. The former is dominated by the imposing **Forte Stella** and **Forte Monte Filippo**; the latter by the ancient **Rocca**, built by Nuno Orejon; it is square in plan with barbicans of Aragonese type.

Here n the photos we see a panorama of Porto Santo Stefano on the day of the **Palio Marinaro** (regatta), and one of Porto Ercole spread out around its beautiful bay with its little port. A panoramic road links the two towns, offering incomparable views.

Well worth while is a tour right round the peninsula and an excursion to the **Grotta dei Santi**, a cave situated in the southern cliff-face. Boats depart daily from Porto Santo Stefano for the Island of Giglio and the nearby Island of Giannutri. The picturesque little town of Giglio Castelli, in spite of tourist development, has preserved intact its medieval character, both in the forms and colours of its architecture. At Giannutri, on the other hand, what is particularly striking are the remains of a **Roman Patrician Villa** of the 1st century A.D.: it probably belonged to Domitius Enobarbus.

On the littoral facing Porto Santo Stefano is the ancient little seaside town of Talamone, a solitary fortified settlement dominated by its castle, the **Rocca del Vecchietta**. The nearby Ansedonia is another wellknown resort spread over the slopes of the promontory of the same name, to the south of the lagoon of Orbetello. On its summit are visible the remains of walls and of public buildings belonging to the ancient city of Cosa (3rd century B.C.). On the shore is the famous **Tagliata Etrusca**, a canal cut through the living rock; close by is a deep cavern (**the Spacco della Regina**) in which, according to legend, Cabiri priests performed mysterious and cruel rites. The seashore is a succession of beaches of silicon sand, hemmed by thick pinewoods and cliffs eroded into caverns.

A few minutes to the west of Grosse-

Porto Santo Stefano.

153

Porto Ercole - view of the port with the old town in the background.

to is its outlet on the sea, Marina di Grosseto, a modern and crowded beach resort, stretched out along a large beach on the edge of an extensive pinewood.

A little further to the north, amid the blue of the sea and the green of the hills and the pinewoods is **Castiglione della Pescaia**. A town of Roman origins, it is linked to the Middle Ages by the power of the most important Pisan families, notably the Gherardesca. Its characteristic portcanal is thronged with pleasure boats and fishing vessels. A modern and renowed bathing resort of international fame, it has numerous well-organized camping sites hidden away in the beautiful pinewoods that surround it. Particularly interesting is its medieval quarter or **Borgo Castello**, huddled within a circuit of massive walls and bastions of the Pisan period. It is dominated by the **Castle** or **Aragonese Fortress** (14th-15th century), whose ramparts drop sheer to the sea.

After passing the locality of **Rocchette** with its medieval castle, we reach Riva del Sole.

Right: *Talamone - the Fort.*
Below: *Talamone - general view.*

RIVA DEL SOLE

This highly modern holiday village was built in the Sixties on the initiative of a Swedish organization, but it is open to any tourist who wants to stay there. Equipped with a large hotel and numerous villas hidden amid dense pinewoods facing the sea, Riva del Sole is a valid example of the adaptation of man to the landscape, enhanced by flower-bordered avenues, shrubberies and well tended lawns, as well as with such facilities as bars, restaurants and swimming pools. The spacious beach differs from those of other nearby resorts, because it consists of sand dunes.

From the coastal road by way of the Via delle Colacchie, then turning left, we can reach **Punta Ala** on a short promontory. This is an elegant residential centre comprising villas, hotels, leisure and sports facilities. The landscape is very varied: apart from its enchanting beaches with jagged rock outcrops between them, its landscape consists of pinewoods woodland and green meadows. Punta Ala is equipped with a modern port designed exclusively for tourist boats. Important annual events are held there, such as a Horse Show, motorboat races, and international conferences of a scientific and cultural character.

A few ancient **Towers** have been converted into modern homes in this area. Particularly interesting is the tower raised on the **Island of Troia** by Jacopo degli Appiani in 1560.

FOLLONICA

Situated on the broad blue gulf to which it has given its name, Follonica is the northernmost bathing resort of the riviera of Grosseto. It is a town of Roman origin which has undergone growing tourist development in recent years. Facing the Gulf of Follonica, which stretches between Punta Ala and Piombino, rises the jagged profile of the **Island of Elba**. To

the north, along the shores of sand dunes and pines, are a number of modern tourist villages such as the Golfo del Sole, Baia Toscana and Lido dei Pini. Of notable interest here are some architectural and decorative features due to the architect Carlo Reishammer, and dating to the period 1831-40; they include the magnificent **Entrance Gate** to the former Iron Foundry, established by the Grand-Ducal government and reactivated by Leopold II in 1834. Equally interesting is the **Parish Church of San Leopoldo** (1836-38), situated at the beginning of the town, in which cast iron, stone, plaster and wood are combined in an unusual way, especially in the pronaos, bell-tower, balustrade and pulpoit. By night, at Follonica, the lights of the waterfront reflected on the sea and the silence seem to arouse a sense of mystery, broken only by the rythmical breaking of the waves on the shore. From on top of one of the modern buildings our gaze sweeps over the long beach of the town and the gulf beyond.

MASSA MARITTIMA

Situated on a hill in the northern part of the Maremma, this little town is probably of Etruscan origin. Thanks to the exploitation of its mineral deposits, "Massa Metallorum" (as it was known) enjoyed a period of economic prosperity and political independence during the Middle Ages: the famous Grossetan Mining Code, the first example of mining legislation in Europe, dates to 1225; concepts that still remain valid today on the ownership of the subsoil are expressed in it. Later, mining activity underwent a decline and was abandoned at the end of the 14th century. Thereafter Massa formed part of the Sienese Republic and was incorporated with it, two centuries later, into the Grand-Duchy of Tuscany. The exploitation of the mines was not resumed until 1830, but at the present time their economic importance is unfortunately progressively decreasing. The historic and artistic centre of the town is formed by an irregular but wonderful piazza, flanked by an exceptional complex of civil and religious buildings. First and foremost is the 13th century **Cathedral**, rising majestically over its high flight of steps. Built in a mixed Romanesque-Gothic style, it has a luminous interior, with a nave and two aisles. To the right is the ancient **Baptistery**. Its Font is the work of Giroldo da Como (1267). It consists of a rectangular basin formed of a single piece of travertine bearing magnificent relief of *Scenes from the Life of the Baptist*. The city museum, **the Museo Comunale** contains numerous archaeological finds and paintings by Sassetta, Sano di Pietro and others, includingg the famous "*Maestà*" of Ambrogio Lorenzetti.

Facing the **Duomo** are such Romanesque buildings as the **Palazzo Pretorio**, ancient residence of the Podestà, the **House of the Counts of Biserno** and the massive **Palazzo Comunale**, formed by the amalgamation of preexisting tower-houses. Of great interest is also the fortified nucleus comprising the ancient clock tower, the **Torre del Candeliere** or **Torre dell'Orologio**, joined by an archway to the new Fortress erected by the Sienese after their conquest of the city.

SOVANA and PITIGLIANO

Sovana is situated in the very heart of the Maremma; it has been dubbed "Jeremiah's town" due to its slow destruction. A former Etruscan city, then capital of the Aldobrandeschi, Sovana is a solitary place, apparently frozen in time. The bas-reliefs of its tombs recall the myths of Ulysses and mythological monsters; its churches, the deep faith of the Middle Ages; its Castle, the strength of the family that dominated it. In the vicinity of the town is the **Etruscan Necropolis**, which is of interest not just for its tombs: the green of the vegetation, the yellow of the rock, the silence and solitude of the place, create profound and unforgettable impressions. The Necropolis consists mainly of chamber tombs hewn in the rock. Especially striking are the remains of the monumental Ildebranda Tomb, in the form of a temple with columns, and the Tomb of the Siren.

Pitigliano, another Etruscan and later Roman city, is situated not far from Sovana. In the Middle Ages it belonged first to the Aldobrandeschi and then (from 1293) to the Orsini, who made it the capital of their territory. The houses of the town are built right to the edge of the high cliffs of tufa on which it stands, riddled with numerous caves, and form an uninterrupted rampart, exemplifying a typically medieval form of urbanism. The central Piazza della Repubblica is dominated by the 14th century **Palazzo degli Orsini**, while facing onto the Piazza Gregorio VII is the handsome façade of the **Cathedral** (13th century), flanked by a massive bell-tower, whose large bronze bell weighs over three tons.

Sovana - Piazza del Pretorio.

MOUNT AMIATA

A conspicuous landmark, both in altitude and geological formation, among the rounded hills of the country of Grosseto and Siena is formed by the volcanic cone of Monte Amiata (1738 m.).

Its flanks are clad in beech and pine firwoods, and dotted with a number of ancient and picturesque villages. In the province of Grosseto the first is Casteldelpiano, of ancient origin, feud of the Abbey of San Salvatore and later of the Aldobrandeschi of Santa Fiora, before passing under Sienese control in 1330.

Not far away is the little hilltown of Arcidosso, a typically medieval settlement huddled round its **Rocca**, but with its modern part scattered over the hills in its immediate environs.

It is followed by Santa Fiora, which developed round its Aldobrandeschi castle. Its beautiful **Parish Church** contains some fine examples of **Glazed Terracotta** attributed to Andrea della Robbia (15th century).

Circling the cone of Monte Amiata, in the eastern part that belongs to the province of Siena, we come to Piancastagnaio with its fortress (Rocca) and fascinating medieval quarter; then **the Abbey of San Salvatore**, round which the little town of Abbadia San Salvatore has developed. At an altitude of 812 m., this is the most important centre of Monte Amiata.

It too has its fortified **Medieval Quarter**. The Abbey itself was founded in the 8th but reconstructed in the 13th century.

It has a very interesting crypt, recently restored to its original appearance. An important mining town noted for the extraction of mercury, Abbadia, like all the other towns of Amiata already mentioned, is a popular summer resort and winter sports centre.

On the summit of Monte Amiata, a monumental wroughtiron **Cross** has been raised; 22 metres high, it was constructed in 1900, and inaugurated on 19 September 1910.

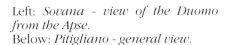

Left: *Sovana - view of the Duomo from the Apse.*
Below: *Pitigliano - general view.*